SCM STUDYGUIDE TO CHRISTIAN MISSION

Historic Types and Contemporary Expressions

Stephen Spencer

scm press

Scripture quotations are from the New Revised Standard Version of
the Bible, copyright 1989 by the Division of Christian Education of
the National Council of the Churches of Christ in the USA. Used by
permission. All rights reserved.

British Library Cataloguing in Publication data

A catalogue record for this book is available from the British Library

978 0 334 04108 5

First published in 2007 by SCM Press
9–17 St Alban's Place,
London N1 0NX

www.scm-canterburypress.co.uk

SCM Press is a division of
SCM-Canterbury Press Ltd

Typeset by Regent Typesetting, London
Printed and bound in Great Britain by
Biddles Ltd, King's Lynn, Norfolk

Contents

Preface

This is not a history of missionary work or a guide to the practicalities of being a missionary but an introduction to the predominant ways the Christian community has understood and practised mission. It does this by identifying a number of 'types' of mission which have emerged through Christian history and which continue to be influential in different parts of the Christian world today. In adopting this approach it follows in the tradition of Max Weber (1864–1920) who developed the notion of *ideal types*, which he described as 'analytical constructs that enable us to simplify a set of social relationships, to detail what is relevant and exclude misleading complexities' (in Graham, Walton and Ward, *Theological Reflection: Methods*, SCM Press 2005, p. 11). A type, then, is a concept which helps to identify and understand the essential features of a more complicated phenomenon. Ernst Troeltsch used this approach to describe the life of the churches, identifying two basic types – the church type and the sect type. A number of other writers have followed his example, adapting and extending it, most recently Elaine Graham, Heather Walton and Frances Ward in relation to theological reflection (ibid., especially pp. 11–12). This book uses this approach to introduce Christian mission. It draws on the work of Hans Küng and David J. Bosch, especially on the six historical paradigms of Christian life and mission that they describe, and out of these it develops and presents six 'types of mission'. It does this through a number of historical portraits which are indicative and exemplary of the development of each type.

This *Studyguide*, then, seeks to provide an overview of different approaches to mission, an overview in which contemporary views and practices can be located and understood. It does this especially for those working at undergraduate Levels 1–2, though the book is also aimed at a wider audience of any in the

Church or society who wish to gain an understanding of the varied and creative ways in which the Church has engaged in mission.

Within each main chapter the book introduces a mission type in four ways. It looks at its sources within wider theological, philosophical and cultural movements. It presents a range of theologians, church leaders and movements who illustrate each one, choosing those who provide the most vivid examples. It presents other more recent examples of each type to show its continuing presence within the Christian community. Finally, it engages in some debate about which of them is the most consistent with the mission of Jesus as a predominant strand of contemporary biblical scholarship presents it.

This last task means there is an ongoing enquiry which runs through the book, an enquiry into which mission type is the most Christ-like within contemporary understanding. And the outcome of this enquiry will help those engaged in mission today to identify and inhabit that type. Some might argue that all the types should be adopted and inhabited by the contemporary Church. This may be possible at a regional or national level but at local level, where churches have limited resources and are best advised to do one thing well rather than six things poorly, choices must be made. This *Studyguide* is intended to help with the making of those choices. So, despite the opening sentence above, the book *does* have a practical application.

A student approaching the subject of missiology for the first time might feel bewildered by a subject that seems to be about every aspect of Christianity and, therefore, no aspect in particular. The first introductory part of the book seeks to prevent this by charting one of a possible number of routes into the subject. It draws on recent historical theology, systematic theology and biblical studies, arguing for a specific way of understanding and practising mission. It is intended only to open up the field of enquiry and to reflect the nature of a discipline which is currently in a provisional, unsettling but exciting place where God's will must be sought amidst the questions and traumas of our time.

The writing of this *Studyguide* would not have been possible without the creative contributions of students in the Carlisle and Blackburn Diocesan Training Institute (between 1999 and 2003) and on the Northern Ordination Course (from 2003 until now) who have been members of my mission theology classes and have helped form my thinking in this broad discipline. I would like to record my immense gratitude to all of them for their contributions.

Christopher Burdon and Stephen Platten have provided invaluable help in reading drafts of different chapters and suggesting corrections and improvements. I am very grateful to them and take responsibility for all the errors and obscurities that remain in the text.

I would like to record my thanks to Barbara Laing and the editorial board at SCM Press for providing the opportunity to write this *Studyguide* and for the encouragement to do so.

My wife Sally has helped me understand and appreciate parts of the Christian tradition which otherwise would have remained misunderstood and unappreciated. She has also read through the entire book suggesting corrections and improvements. In gratitude for this and for much else these pages are dedicated to her with love.

Part 1

Orientation

There is in God – some say –
A deep, but dazzling darkness; as men here
Say it is late and dusky, because they
See not all clear.

(Henry Vaughan, 'The Night')

1

Mission in Crisis

It is fifty years since Mrs Rosa Parks, a black tailor's assistant in a city centre department store in Montgomery, Alabama, in the deep south of the United States, boarded a bus and took a seat. When the bus filled up the driver ordered Mrs Parks to stand so that a white man could sit down. She refused to move: 'She'd gone shopping after work, and her feet hurt. She couldn't bear the thought of having to stand all the way home. The driver, of course, threatened to call the police. Go ahead and call them, Mrs Parks sighed. And she thought how you spend your whole life making things comfortable for white people. You just live for their well-being, and they don't even treat you like a human being. Well, let the cops come. She wasn't moving' (Oats 1982, pp. 64–5).

Mrs Parks was arrested and charged. She found support, though, from the NAACP (National Association for the Advancement of Colored People), and especially from one of its leaders in Montgomery, a young Baptist minister called Martin Luther King Jnr. He and other members of the association decided to call for a boycott of the bus company by the black community. Over forty church ministers and community leaders met in one of the city churches and gave their support to the idea. The boycott was launched a couple of days later and the response from the black community was unanimous – the buses were empty the following morning.

This was the start of a protracted campaign, involving legal battles in court and rallying calls to the community to maintain the boycott. The campaign reached far into 1956, stirring up intense opposition in sections of the white community and periods of worry in the NAACP that the campaign would fail. King himself was arrested and fined at one point. But he was quite clear from the start that the protests were to be peaceful and to 'be guided by the deepest principles of the Christian faith. Love must be our regulating ideal . . .' The response from the black community was emphatic and the campaign became the defining moment of King's life. He became a national celebrity, travelling across the United States to speak about the protest and drum up support. But the authorities in Montgomery were as defiant as ever and in early November succeeded in getting a judge to rule that the car pool, which black people had been using instead of the buses, was 'a public nuisance' and therefore illegal. After almost twelve months it seemed as if the protest had failed. But, at that very same moment, the Supreme Court in Washington ruled that the local laws in Alabama requiring segregation of races were unconstitutional. It was victory at last, a turning point in the way black people were regarded in the south and, indeed, across the country. The implementation of the ruling would take further struggle, especially when some black churches were blown up by white supremacists, but a threshold had been crossed.

Mission as social action

Why remember these events on their fiftieth anniversary? One reason is that at a time when many in the churches are looking for new ways to give mission expression (in response to ongoing decline in church attendance), these events vividly embody one form of missionary engagement. When many churches are drawing up mission strategies and action plans it is possible that Rosa Parks, the NAACP and Martin Luther King suggest an inspiring (and challenging) way forward.

According to this view mission is about the coming of the kingdom of God, with its peace and justice and healing, to the dark places of the world. The work of the Church is to assist this wider mission in whatever ways it can, such as through supporting the civil rights movement in 1950s America. It is about Christians coming out of their bunkers and marching alongside others for an end to poverty and oppression. Whether or not the Church grows or declines is secondary to this. In words often attributed to Archbishop William Temple, the Church of God is the only institution that exists to serve the needs of those who are not its members, so Christian mission is about assisting with what God is doing in the world: mission *is* human development.

But is this the right approach? How can God's mission be assisted if there does not already exist a vibrant Church to do the assisting? How can his mission even be *identified* if his people are not gathering in church week by week to hear that mission described in the reading of Scripture? If significant energies are not devoted to building up the internal life of the Church how will it avoid losing itself in the struggles of the world? (See Chapter 9 for further discussion of this approach.)

Mission as church growth

A different outlook is found in the recent Church of England report *Mission-Shaped Church*. In its longest and most detailed chapter it provides a description of different kinds of congregational church life, which it describes as 'fresh expressions of church'. It lists among others the following: alternative worship communities, café and cell churches, churches arising out of community initiatives, mid-week congregations, network churches, school-based congregations, church plants and traditional forms inspiring new interest. The report suggests that these are 'a sign of the creativity of the Spirit in our age . . . a sign of the work of God and of the kingdom' (Cray *et al.* 2004, p. 80).

The assumption in all this is that the mission of God is primarily concerned with forming these various kinds of church meeting: mission *is* growing the Church. This is actually stated at different points in the report, such as in the introduction: 'the church is the fruit of God's mission . . . creating new communities of Christian faith is part of the mission of God to express God's kingdom in every geographic and cultural context' (ibid. p. xii).

But is it? Some of the initiatives, such as alternative worship services and network churches, have been described as maintenance rather than mission, a kind of chaplaincy to those who cannot bring themselves to attend traditional churches any more. It is questioned whether such initiatives have drawn new people into the life of the Church. Some of the other initiatives have been described as serving the wishes of the world rather than God, serving coffee and cake rather than Christ. Other initiatives, like the school-based congregations, have often been supported by parents who wish to win a place for their child in a church school, but when the child starts at the new school the parents, more often than not, stop coming to the church. They seem to lack commitment, which questions whether real mission has taken place. Overall, there appear to be a number of uncomfortable features of 'fresh expressions of church' when these initiatives are viewed as mission. (See further Hull 2006. For discussion of a church-centred view of mission see Chapter 5.)

Mission as public witness

A third point of view seeks to have the best of both worlds. It agrees that mission is *not* primarily about bringing people into church, which is putting the cart before the horse. But nor is mission about the Church losing itself in wider struggles for a better world: if Christ is not named and not known in missionary work then *Christian mission* does not take place. He is the way, the truth and the life and only through him can true salvation be achieved. Mission is about proclaiming Christ in the world and churches need to follow his example and be bold and adventurous in this. They are to gear their activities to spreading the news about Jesus along the highways and hedgerows of society: mission *is* proclamation. A recent advocate of this view was Lesslie Newbigin, who in *The Gospel in a Pluralist Society* called for the churches in the West to engage in the mission task of proclaiming the gospel as 'Public Truth': 'in Christ we have been shown the road. We cannot treat that knowledge as a private matter for ourselves. It concerns the whole human family' (Newbigin 1989, p. 183). An example of this kind of proclamation would be recent attempts to increase the provision of state-funded church schools across Britain with their explicit commitment to teaching the Christian faith. (For discussion of church/state mission see Chapter 7.)

Who is right? The differences between these three influential views are profound. There are other significant points of view as well, not least the traditional evangelical view which sees evangelism as the defining feature of mission (see Stott 1986; see also Kirk 2006; for discussion see Chapter 8). Other distinct views from Christian history also demand attention. One thing is certain, that there is a general lack of agreement about the nature of mission. David Bosch, in his encyclopedic survey of thinking about mission, *Transforming Mission*, published 25 years ago and still definitive for the subject as a whole, stated that the loose use of the word 'mission' in the last half-century masked a crisis (Bosch 1991, p. 1): he believed there had been a terrible failure of nerve over mission (ibid., p. 7) and that the churches were not sure any more what it was really all about. Twenty-five years later, with mission understood in an ever increasing number of ways in the churches, reflecting an increasingly pluralist society, it seems the crisis is far from over. Furthermore, the word itself has been adopted by industry and commerce to describe its own variegated attempts to make money, with 'mission statements' appearing in every corporate reception area. It has become an overused and undervalued word.

What, then, are the churches to do within this 'deep, but dazzling darkness'? In one place Bosch recalled that in Chinese the word 'crisis' is spelt with two characters, one standing for 'danger' and the other for 'opportunity'. This suggests that when events take a dangerous turn a moment of opportunity has arrived: new initiatives can be taken, new directions found, hope restored. In this new century the crisis of mission is still upon us, but so is a moment of opportunity.

It seems increasingly clear that local churches need to explore and reflect on the right way to reach out to their surrounding communities. This means they need to ask a basic theological question about the nature of mission, a question which needs to be answered before secondary questions about practice and strategy can be faced. Is mission primarily concerned with engineering church growth, or is the joining of wider struggles for a better world the right way forward, or is the proclamation of the gospel in the public arena the overriding calling?

This *Studyguide* presents a range of answers to this question. It begins by laying out some of the theological groundwork that is needed before looking for an answer, beginning with an exploration of the root meaning of the word 'mission' and its home in the doctrine of the Trinity. It identifies underlying principles of Jesus' own mission in Galilee. It then examines the main historic types of mission in the Christian tradition, seeing how they were forged in the cross-currents of history and culture and how they continue to be expressed by different Christian communities in the present, and it asks how consistent they are with the principles of Jesus' own mission. In these ways it seeks to present the resources that any student will need to work out their own answer to the question 'chat is Christian mission today?'

Discussion questions

How would you describe the essential nature of Christian mission? Which passages of Scripture would you use to expound it?

Further reading

Bosch, David J. (1991), *Transforming Mission: Paradigm Shifts in Theology of Mission*, Orbis

Cray, Graham, *et al.* (2004), *Mission-Shaped Church: Church Planting and Fresh Expressions of Church in a Changing Context*, Church House Publishing

Hull, John M. (2006), *Mission-Shaped Church: A Theological Response*, SCM Press

Kirk, J. Andrew (2006), *Mission Under Scrutiny: Confronting Current Challenges*, DLT

Newbigin, Lesslie (1989), *The Gospel in a Pluralist Society*, SPCK

Oats, Stephen B. (1982), *Let the Trumpet Sound: The Life of Martin Luther King Jnr*, HarperCollins

Stott, John (1986), *Christian Mission in the Modern World*, Kingsway

Note: The titles in the 'Further reading' lists through this book are publications mentioned in the text and a few others. The lists provide starting points for exploration of the relevant topics but are not intended to be comprehensive guides to all the relevant literature. Such guidance needs to be sought through the bibliographies found in the titles that are listed.

2

Origins of a Word
Mission as *Missio Dei*

When a walker becomes lost in the fells, they are wise to turn around and look back along the route from which they have just come. This will involve pausing on the journey, which may be frustrating, but it allows them to work out the direction in which they are heading. In a similar way this *Studyguide* is an attempt to help those engaged in mission to pause and turn and look back along the route from which they have come, so that they may have a clearer idea of where they are going.

A good way of beginning to do this is to ask how the use of the word 'mission' itself has evolved. An analysis of its genealogy reveals that before the sixteenth century it was not used to describe an aspect of church life but was found in a different context, to describe relationships within the holy Trinity. The Latin word 'missio', meaning 'to send', was used to describe the sending of the Son by the Father, and also of the sending of the Holy Spirit by the Father and the Son (Bosch 1991, p. 390). An early example is from the eucharistic prayer of Hippolytus, whose earliest extant version is in Latin and dates from the years 215–17 AD. In this prayer the Father is thanked for his beloved Son Jesus Christ 'whom in your good pleasure you sent from heaven into the womb of a virgin . . .' (in Evans and Wright 1991, p. 15). Another example comes from the Latin Vulgate translation of Romans 8.2: 'for God . . . by sending his own son . . .'.

In the late sixteenth and early seventeenth centuries it was the Jesuits in Latin America who started to use the term in a more restricted sense, changing its subject matter from divine to human agency. They started to use it to describe the spreading of the Christian faith among the heathen of that continent and, subsequently, of the spreading of the Counter-Reformation Catholic faith among the Protestants of Europe. (See Neill 1964, pp. 202–4 for a description of the Jesuits in Paraguay.)

In the nineteenth century the word began to be used in an even more restricted sense, to describe the sending not of the whole Christian faith but of certain representatives of it, specifically the sending of missionaries to a designated territory where they would preach the gospel and convert non-Christian people. It was in this sense that the word was used in the naming of the new Church Missionary Society in 1801. This became the modern understanding of the term and is still used in the media and popular culture generally to this day.

Today, after the colonization of vast areas of the globe by the European powers in the nineteenth and early twentieth centuries, with the complicity of the churches in that whole process, there is embarrassment about the word and the desire of many to abandon it: if *that* is mission then we want no more part of it.

But the Trinitarian roots of the word are a reminder that mission is about much more than what the churches attempt to achieve or fail to achieve.

Karl Barth

In the twentieth century, through the influence of the Swiss theologian Karl Barth (1886–1968) and his 'crisis theology', with its stress on the primacy of God's initiative in salvation history, the churches have rediscovered a deeper and richer meaning to the word (Barth is more fully introduced in Chapter 10). Barth's insight into the nature of mission came about at one of the lowest points of the twentieth century when the Nazis were about to come to power and any confidence in the idea of human progress finally evaporated. At that time Barth was teaching in Germany and knew very well what the rise of the Nazis meant for Europe (and for his own position in Germany). Nevertheless, when he addressed the Brandenburg Missionary Conference of 1932, a gathering of missionaries and theologians, he described Christian mission in defiant phrases as

a will and an order that does not conform to any system made up of human understanding, points of view, or reasons, even if these were made by the most enlightened Christians. Is not this free will and order something ever new, and always with the courage to begin anew, as read in Holy Scripture, as heard, and as understood? Its content may be an imperative to 'go forward', or 'stop', or 'go back!' Yet, no matter what, it indicates that we cannot will to be self-sufficient, but must always be open and prepared to find it. (Quoted in Thomas 1995, p. 106)

After the war, in 1952, when the churches were once again contemplating a renewal of mission at the Willingen Conference of the International Missionary Council, Barth's influence took hold and his insight was expressed and developed in the conference resolution. It makes an explicit and important connection between church missionary work and the nature of God as Trinity:

The missionary movement of which we are a part has its source in the Triune God himself. Out of the depths of his love for us, the Father has sent forth his own beloved Son to reconcile all things to himself . . . We who have been chosen in Christ . . . are committed to full participation in his redeeming mission. There is no participation in Christ without participation in his mission to the world. That by which the Church receives its existence is that by which it is also given its world-mission. (Quoted in Avis 2005, p. 5)

This was a highly significant moment in the genealogy of the word 'mission' because it was reconnecting it with its early Christian roots in the doctrine of the Trinity. It led to the widespread adoption in ecumenical circles of the Latin term *missio Dei* to describe the real meaning of mission. Paul Avis unpacks its meaning:

The Latin term is necessary because it holds a depth and power that English translation cannot capture: the mission of God, the mission that belongs to God, the mission that flows from the heart of God. *Missio Dei* speaks of the overflowing of the love of God's being and nature into God's purposeful activity in the world. (Avis 2005, p. 5)

Mission, then, can be understood to be all about the *missio Dei*, God's initiative in creating and redeeming the world. It is an outpouring of love that began with his words 'Let there be light' and continued with the diverse wonders of the six days of creation. It is a sending of love that continued with the calling of Abram and the birth of the people of Israel through the patriarchs. It continued with the story of the people being called out of slavery in Egypt, being offered the covenant as they travelled through the wilderness and were led into the promised land. God's fatherly love was expressed through the sending of the prophets, the punishment of the exile and the restoration of the people to their land.

Then, above all, it found expression in the sending of his Son, 'for God so loved the world that he sent his only son . . .'. The birth, life and death of Christ was the supreme expression of God's mission, for this was where the depths of his love for his world were revealed, above all on the cross. The outcome of this outpouring was the rising again of Christ on the third day, his appearing to the disciples and many others, and then the sending of the Holy Spirit to empower and equip the disciples for spreading the good news about all of this. The completion of the *missio Dei* is awaited at the end of all things, when the love of God will bring all things into the perfection, peace and joy of the life of the holy Trinity once more.

'Mission' therefore is not 'the Church going out and saving people'. Rather, it is *God creating and saving the world*, and this includes not only creating and saving people but the natural world and indeed cosmos as a whole. It is therefore something immensely greater than the Church. It is the primary fact, and the Church is secondary: the mission of God came first, and the Church was created as a response to that. So the Church is a product of mission, rather than the other way round. As Emil Brunner reputedly put it, 'the Church exists by mission just as fire exists by burning'. Mission, as Bosch writes, 'is thereby seen as a movement from God to the world; the church is viewed as an instrument for that mission . . . To participate in mission is to participate in the movement of God's love toward people, since God is a fountain of sending love' (Bosch 1991, p. 390).

What does this imply for the work of the Church? Bosch writes that Christian missionary activity

> can not simply be the planting of churches or the saving of souls; rather, it has to be service of the *missio Dei*, representing God in and over against the world, pointing to God, holding up the God-child before the eyes of the world in a ceaseless celebration of the Feast of the Epiphany. In its mission,

the church witnesses to the fullness of the promise of God's reign and participates in the ongoing struggle between that reign and the powers of darkness and evil. (1991, p. 391)

During the 1960s and 1970s there was further development in this understanding. These years saw a growing realization that the *missio Dei* should not be restricted to the Church's sphere of influence.

Since God's concern is for the entire world, this should also be the scope of the *missio Dei*. It affects all people in all aspects of their existence. Mission is God's turning to the world in respect of creation, care, redemption and consummation . . . It takes place in ordinary human history, not exclusively in and through the church . . . The *missio Dei* is God's activity, which embraces both the church and the world, and in which the church may be privileged to participate. (Bosch 1991, p. 391)

Vatican II

The Second Vatican Council, the reforming and modernizing council of all the Roman Catholic bishops that met in Rome between 1962 and 1965, brought this thinking into the heart of the Roman Catholic Church. In its rousing decree on the Church's missionary activity (*Ad Gentes*), a key document of the Council, it stated that

The church on earth is by its very nature missionary since, according to the Father, it has its origin in the mission of the Son and the Holy Spirit. This plan flows from 'fountain-like love,' the love of God the Father . . . Missionary activity is nothing else, and nothing less, than the manifestation of God's plan, its epiphany and realization in the world and in history; that by which God, through mission, clearly brings to its conclusion the history of salvation. Through preaching and the celebration of the sacraments, of which the holy Eucharist is the centre and summit, missionary activity makes Christ present, who is the author of salvation. (*Ad Gentes* 2, 9, in *Vatican Council II*, pp. 444, 453)

But mission is not restricted to the Church: God's saving activity is at work in the world as well as the Church, especially through the secret moving of the Spirit in human beings, advancing the salvation of people through love. And such secretive work may, by the grace of God, issue in a more humane world. So *Gaudium et Spes*, Vatican II's 'Pastoral constitution on the Church in the modern world', speaks of human progress in creating a more just social order in the modern world. It then declares,

> The Spirit of God, who, with wondrous providence, directs the course of time and renews the faith of the earth, assists at this development . . . such progress is of vital concern to the kingdom of God, in so far as it can contribute to the better ordering of human society. (*Gaudium et Spes* 26, 39, in *Vatican Council II*, pp. 192, 204; quoted in Bosch 1991, p. 392)

Conclusion

The recognition that mission is God's mission represents a crucial breakthrough in respect of the preceding centuries (Bosch 1991, p. 393). It transforms the whole way in which mission is viewed and liberates the Church from trying to depend upon its own limited resources. It is the starting point for the explorations of this *Studyguide*. It also allows us to return to the quotation which began this section of the book, from the poem 'The Night' by the Welsh poet Henry Vaughan (1622–95), which spoke of a 'deep, but dazzling darkness' where 'not all [was] clear'. These words were quoted because they describe well the contemporary crisis of understanding over mission in the churches. But Vaughan's verse goes on to welcome this night time because it allows him to enter into union with God:

> O for that Night! Where I in Him
> Might live invisible and dim!

The churches, now, might welcome the night of crisis for mission because it has allowed them to rediscover the way authentic mission springs from God himself. They now know they are fundamentally dependent on life 'in him' and that this Trinitarian life can liberate them from having to rely upon their own weak resources.

Discussion questions

Can you detect the Spirit of God at work in the secular world? Describe some examples.

How do these signs of the *missio Dei* develop or change your understanding of the mission of the Church?

Further reading

Avis, Paul (2005), *A Ministry Shaped by Mission*, T & T Clark

Bosch, David J. (1991), *Transforming Mission: Paradigm Shifts in Theology of Mission*, Orbis

Evans, G. R., and J. Robert Wright (1991), *The Anglican Tradition: A Handbook of Sources*, SPCK

Moltmann, Jürgen (1977), *The Church in the Power of the Spirit*, SCM Press

Neill, Stephen (1964), *A History of Christian Missions*, Penguin

Thomas, Norman, ed. (1995), *Readings in World Mission*, SPCK

Vatican Council II: The Basic Sixteen Documents (1996), ed. Austin Flannery OP, Dominican Publications

3

Digging Deeper
Mission as Participation
in the Trinity

The walker who is lost in the fells will not only look back along the route they have come. They will also consult their map, a human document of abstract symbols that represents the key features of the hills and valleys all around. In a similar way, as we seek to get our bearings on the nature of mission, it is worthwhile consulting the maps that have been produced by the Christian community, as it were, because they can direct our attention to the key features of God's mission in the world.

The last chapter established that the Willengen Conference, under the influence of Karl Barth, marked a rediscovery of one very significant map for mission, the doctrine of the Trinity. Since then a number of theologians have explored and interpreted the meaning of this map and drawn out its implications for Christian mission, and to them we now turn.

Background

The doctrine of the Holy Trinity, articulated in the pronouncements of the Councils of Nicaea (325) and Constantinople (381), states that God is three *hypostases* (Greek) / *personae* (Latin) / persons (English), in one *ousia* (Greek) / *substantia* (Latin) / being (English). This doctrine has always been at the heart of belief in the Eastern Orthodox churches but was down-played in the Western Church for many centuries. Friedrich Schleiermacher (1768–1834), the great German Reformed theologian who is often described as 'the father of modern theology', placed the doctrine at the end of his systematic presentation of the Christian faith, almost as an afterword. But theologians over the last 80 years have rediscovered its centrality in a significant way. Karl Barth, whom we have seen to be a pioneer in these matters, argued for the foundational importance of the doctrine of the Trinity to all Christian thinking. He famously placed discussion of the Trinity at the start of his *Church Dogmatics*, reminding the churches that because God has revealed himself as inherently three in one, all theology, ethics, and pastoral work must begin, and end, here.

After the Second World War two Protestant theologians, Wolfhart Pannenberg and especially Jürgen Moltmann, made an important connection between the Trinity and human history. The Trinity was seen as intimately involved within human history through the ministry of Christ: 'It is not the church that has a mission of salvation to fulfil in the world; it is the mission of the Son and the Spirit through the Father that includes the church' (Moltmann 1977, p. 65). Christian mission, then, has its roots in an eternal sending within God, so that participation in one is participation in the other.

But what is the precise connection between the two: *how* is participation in one participation in the other? A number of theologians have recently provided some answers to this question.

Leonardo Boff

Boff is a Roman Catholic Franciscan priest who has worked within the tradition of Latin American liberation theology since the 1980s. He had his licence to teach as a Roman Catholic theologian removed by the Vatican over some of his views. In one of his most famous books he made an explicit connection between the Trinity and human society, suggesting that the perfect relationships of the three equal persons within the one society of God provide a model for human society to strive towards. In *Trinity and Society*, first published in Brazil in 1986, he wrote that, 'The community of Father, Son and Holy Spirit becomes the prototype of the human community dreamed of by those who wish to improve society and build it in such a way as to make it into the image and likeness of the

Trinity.' This revolutionary view sees the Trinity 'as a model for any just, egalitarian (while respecting differences) social organisation. On the basis of their faith in the triune God Christians postulate a society that can be the image and likeness of the Trinity' (Boff 1988, pp. 7, 11).

The missionary role of the Church alongside other groups in society therefore becomes this: to struggle to move the human community away from current unequal relationships of exploitation and oppression and towards this perfect kind of society, a society like the society of the divine Trinity.

Catherine Mowry LaCugna

LaCugna, on the other hand, an American Catholic theologian who published *God for Us: The Trinity and Christian Life* in 1991, did not see the Trinity as presenting a template for society but as issuing an invitation to enter a relationship. She has become an influential figure in the renewal of understanding of the Trinity. She built her understanding on the insight that persons are not isolated self-contained entities but beings *in relationship*, who exist for communion. She believed that human life expressed its true nature and meaning when persons come together in a loving fellowship, and the essential meaning of the Trinity is that God reaches out to the world in Christ, through the power and presence of the Spirit, and invites all people to enter into a loving communion of human and divine persons:

> Trinitarian theology could be described as par excellence a theology of relationship, which explores mysteries of love, relationship, personhood and communion within the framework of God's self-revelation in the person of Christ and the activity of the Spirit. (LaCugna 1991, p. 1)

In the 1990s there have been a number of British theologians who have taken these ideas further, including the late Colin Gunton at King's College London, and David Cunningham in his book *These Three Are One* of 1998. Cunningham also moves from analysis of human personhood and relationships to an exploration of the doctrine of the Trinity, suggesting that the way to fulfilment of persons is through imitation of the Trinity. Cunningham talks about the Trinitarian *virtues* of 'polyphony', 'participation' and 'particularity' which can be lived out in human interaction.

Paul Fiddes

But a recent and important book by the Baptist theologian Paul Fiddes, *Participating in God: A Pastoral Doctrine of the Trinity* (2000), while also seeking to make connections between the doctrine and pastoral practice, does so in a different way. He distances himself from the earlier books by saying he is not looking to the Trinity as a picture of a social group *to imitate*. Such an approach is reductionist – it reduces the otherness and divine mystery of God through trying to conform him to a human image of community (p. 29). Put the other way round, how can a group of human beings begin to represent the utter transcendence and mystery of God?

Fiddes looks to the doctrine of the Trinity not for a picture of a kind of society or community but for an analogy, a point of connection between two very different realities. Drawing on Barth, he says that because God in revelation has 'seized' words to make them capable of meaningful talk about God, 'by God's grace they have been made into analogies which speak truly and reliably about God' (p. 30).

The doctrine of the Trinity, for Fiddes, provides one very special analogy which has not been clearly enough recognized in the recent literature. It is based on the way that Christ has revealed God to be a father, that is, someone who does not exist on his own but only in relationship with a son, who is Jesus himself: it is not possible to be a father without the existence of a child, and it is not possible to be a child without the existence of a parent. Christ has revealed the familial nature of God and therefore of the mutual participation of the persons of the Trinity. This means that within the Trinity there are distinct contributions but unity at the same time. In this kind of relationship the very existence of the distinct contributions depends on their participating in each other's life: you cannot have one without the other.

So he uses a Greek word, *perichoresis*, first used by Pseudo-Cyril in the sixth century, and then by John of Damascus in the eighth century, literally meaning 'around dancing' and more deeply meaning 'reciprocity and exchange in the mutual indwelling of the persons', to express how each person can permeate and coinhere with the others without confusion. There is a *perichoresis* of the persons of the Trinity within the unity of their substance (p. 71).

It is this concept which provides a guiding analogy for human living. It suggests that persons truly exist through their participation in each other. It suggests we should not think of persons *in* relationship, but persons *as* relationship (p. 50). Fiddes wants to get away from a different kind of thinking which tries to observe personal agents on the 'ends' of relationship. Rather, he is seeing persons as *constituted* in 'sharing, in speech and worship, in the flow of relationships themselves' (p. 72) He is recalling a famous point made by the Scottish philosopher John Macmurray in his Gifford Lectures of 1954, *Persons in Relation*, who argued that 'the self is constituted by its relation to the Other; it has its being in its relationships and this relationship is necessarily personal' (see LaCugna 1991, pp. 255–60).

A dance involving two or more people can be an example of this kind of relationship, where the dance is an improvisation formed by the flowing interaction of the dancers (rather than pre-rehearsed set-piece dancing). One of the dancers on their own could not create the dance: it depends on the interaction of all the dancers. But in '*this* dance the partners not only encircle each other and weave in and out between each other as in human dancing; in the divine dance, so intimate is the communion that they move in and through each other so that the pattern is all-inclusive' (Fiddes 2000, p. 72).

So when people are in a relationship with each other, reaching out in friendship, risk, challenge, service, sacrifice, finding a new identity in the sharing of their differences, their lives are being conformed, in one crucial respect, to the life of the Trinity.

But they will not only be *like* God. Fiddes emphasizes that this kind of relationship also allows them to participate *within* God's life itself – they will be *joining the divine interrelationship*. So, speaking of the life of a Christian congregation, he writes that 'communion in the body of Christ is not just a *model* of the Trinity, but a means of *entering* the relational movements of the triune God'. There is a reality of participation which allows the people 'to share in God rather than attempting to observe God'. In other words,

> to understand divine persons as relations is to foster a participative model of the churches . . . To do so, I suggest, is to be drawn into a communion where the saying of 'Amen' by every member becomes a sharing of the Amen of the Son to the Father; so the 'Amen' of the congregation to the liturgy of the eucharist is not simply a passive reception, but an entering into a divine activity which will be expressed as the exercising of a charismatic gift. (Fiddes 2000, pp. 88–9)

This quotation re-establishes a connection with Moltmann who, when talking of the Holy Spirit, described how it was possible for human beings to enter into the divine life:

> The fellowship of the triune God is so open and inviting that it is depicted in the fellowship of the Holy Spirit, which human beings experience with one another – 'as you, Father, are in me and I in you' – and takes this true human fellowship into itself and gives it a share in itself: 'that they may also be *in us*'. (Moltmann 1992, p. 60)

Conclusion

All of this has fundamental implications for mission: 'the mission of God flows directly from the nature of who God is. It is impossible to be more basic than that. God's intention for the world is that in every respect it should show forth the way he is – love, community, equality, diversity, mercy, compassion and justice' (Kirk 1999, p. 28). The doctrine of the Trinity, in other words, 'is not a piece of "high theology" reserved for the professional scholar, but something that has a living, *practical* importance for every Christian' (Kallistos Ware in Bevans and Schroeder 2004, p. 274).

Bevans and Schroeder, in their wide-ranging update of Bosch's *Transforming Mission*, summarize this practical application in the following helpful way:

> The mutual openness of Father and Son, Son and Spirit, Spirit and Father as a model of relationship, the constitutive nature of relationship for personal identity, the inclusion of diversity in community – all these vital truths and practices are rooted in Trinitarian reality and existence. (Bevans and Schroeder 2004, p. 274)

They add that it has been Orthodox theologians like Vladimir Lossky, John Meyendorff and John Zizioulas who have helped theologians in the West understand the Trinity as 'an ec-static communion of persons, always involved in the world, always inviting all of creation to share in the triune life of communion-in-mission' (Bevans and Schroeder 2004, p. 274). It can be added that these writers have themselves been drawing on ancient patristic and mystical writings.

To be part of mission, then, is not just to be an agent, at arm's length, of someone else's project: it is to participate in the very heart of who God is, to be caught up *within* and contribute *to* the interactive and flowing interrelationship of Father, Son and Holy Spirit, a relationship that gives life and gives it abundantly.

Discussion questions

Think of examples of the way different relationships help to constitute you as a person.

How does this affect your understanding of the divinity of Christ?

How does it affect your understanding of mission?

Further reading

Bevans, Stephen B., and Roger P. Schroeder (2004), *Constants in Context: A Theology of Mission for Today*, Orbis

Boff, Leonardo (1988), *Trinity and Society*, Orbis

Bosch, David J. (1991), *Transforming Mission: Paradigm Shifts in Theology of Mission*, Orbis

Cunningham, David (1998), *These Three Are One: The Practice of Trinitarian Theology*, Blackwell

Fiddes, Paul (2000), *Participating in God: A Pastoral Doctrine of the Trinity*, DLT

Kirk, J. Andrew (1999), *What is Mission? Theological Explorations*, DLT

LaCugna, Catherine M. (1991), *God for Us: The Trinity and Christian Life*, Harper

Moltmann, Jürgen (1977), *The Church in the Power of the Spirit*, SCM Press

Moltmann, Jürgen (1992), *History and the Triune God*, SCM Press

4

In Human Terms
The Prophetic Mission
of Christ

The walker who is lost in the fells may draw some comfort from their map, but interpreting the abstract symbols on the paper is not always straightforward. Which hill does one set of gradients represent? What is the meaning of the shaded areas on another part of the map? What do all the tiny dots mean? The walker might well find another document of more use, the guide book. This will be an account, by someone who has walked this way, of what it is actually like from a human and practical point of view to follow this route. The guide book will say when to turn left and when to turn right and when to look up and take in the view.

In a similar way the doctrine of the Trinity, as comprehensive as it is, can only be of limited use as a guide to mission. It is a general and abstract doctrine and cannot answer a key question: *How* in practical terms is the Christian community to engage in mission? *How* is it to serve the flow of God's Trinitarian mission as it reaches out into the actual world with its array of specific needs?

The Fourth Gospel begins to provide one answer to this question when it shows Jesus giving the Holy Spirit to his disciples with the decisive words 'As the Father has sent me, even so I send you' (20.21). His followers, then, are to continue his mission, the mission that he received from his Father. They are to continue doing what he did during his own life: his ministry of teaching, healing, caring, listening and giving of all. So the Church, as the successor of the first disciples who received this commission, is to continue this work.

The question, then, becomes this: what are the key features of Christ's mission that should govern the mission of the Church?

Bearing in mind that Trinitarian mission is all about participative relationship, it is to the ways that Jesus relates to those around him that we must pay attention. We shall not look for a certain kind of institutional life or legal code that must always be present to authenticate mission, but for the distinctive ways he interacted with the people he encountered.

A good place to begin is Jesus' Galilean ministry. This is because the first three Gospels, and especially Mark, make it clear that the Galilean period, before Jesus' journeys further afield with his disciples, was a defining moment in his ministry, a moment in which the kingdom of God drew near. This is seen in Jesus' comment at the last supper when he tells his disciples that after he is raised up he will go ahead of them to Galilee (Mark 14.28): According to Morna Hooker, a recent commentator on Mark, Galilee in Mark's Gospel is 'the centre' of Jesus' ministry and of discipleship, in contrast to Jerusalem, which is the place of suffering (Hooker 1991, p. 345). Also, after the resurrection the messenger in the tomb says to the women to go and tell the disciples and Peter that Jesus is going ahead of them to Galilee (16.7): Galilee is to be the place where the resurrection is witnessed, which means the Galilean ministry of healing and feeding the crowds and preaching the gospel is being resurrected with renewed vigour. The Galilean ministry is therefore paradigmatic of the whole of Christ's missionary enterprise.

A survey of this ministry can begin with Mark 1.14–45. This is because this passage provides a summary of how Jesus went about his preaching and healing in Galilee (Myers 1988, p. 149). In its pole position, in what is generally regarded as the first written Gospel, it becomes a keynote chapter, introducing a whole range of missionary encounters between Jesus and a variety of different people. It provides an overview of what Jesus did and said before his ministry became dominated by the growing opposition of the religious authorities.

The first two verses (vv. 14–15), describing his entry into Galilee, are a good place to begin. They provide an initial and defining expression of his mission, acting as a summary of all that follows. It is important to spend some time analysing the nature of this entry:

Now after John was arrested, Jesus came into Galilee, preaching the gospel of God, and saying, 'The time is fulfilled, and the kingdom of God is at hand; repent, and believe in the gospel.' (Mark 1.14–15)

Jesus' words make clear that the subject of his ministry is not to be his own rise to power or glorification; he is not launching a campaign centred on himself and his own authority. Instead he is launching a campaign about something much wider and bigger – a new reality that is beginning to break into the life of the world, namely the coming of the kingdom of God. Jesus points away from himself to this overarching reality. All that he says and does is not an end in itself but a pointer or sign to what God is doing universally. He is taking up the role of a herald, one who goes around announcing a forthcoming event. One commentator expresses all this in the following way:

> Everything that Jesus says and does is inspired from beginning to end by his personal commitment to the coming Reign of God into the world. The controlling horizon of the mission and ministry of Jesus is the Kingdom of God. The life, death and resurrection of Jesus derive their meaning from the announcement of the Kingdom of God. (Knitter 1996, p. 89)

But he is not just announcing something. He also calls for a personal response among his listeners: they are to 'repent and believe'. He calls on the people to change the direction of their lives, as John the Baptist had been doing, and prepare for the coming of the kingdom. So he is combining a 'macro' dimension, of announcing God's will and purpose for the nation and the world, with a 'micro' dimension, of calling for a change of consciousness and outlook in people's own hearts and lives.

How can this dynamic and complex interaction be characterized as a whole? What kind of role was he expressing? Was he primarily a rabbi figure, teaching a new kind of wisdom, or a political figure, canvassing for a change in government, or a healer and exorcist, bringing healing to individual people's lives? The figures in the Old Testament who both announced God's forthcoming purposes for the people *and* called on them to respond in their hearts were, of course, the prophets. They also combined a 'macro' dimension, of announcing God's will and purpose for the nation and the world, with a 'micro' dimension, of calling for a change of consciousness and outlook within the lives and hearts of their listeners. Walter Brueggemann's famous definition of prophetic ministry, based on his own extensive studies of Old Testament prophecy, expresses this well:

> The task of prophetic ministry is to nurture, nourish, and evoke a consciousness and perception alternative to the consciousness and perception of the

dominant culture around us . . . [it] serves to criticize in dismantling the dominant consciousness . . . [and it] serves to energize persons and communities by its promise of another time and situation toward which the community of faith may move. (Brueggemann 2001, p. 3)

Jesus, it seems clear from the first chapter of Mark, was taking up this type of role: his ministry was to be a *prophetic* one.

Other Gospels and commentators

Many passages from the Gospels confirm this by making clear how his contemporaries saw him as a prophet: Matt. 16.14 / Mark 8.28 / Luke 9.19; Luke 9.7. See also Mark 6.15; Matt. 21.11; Luke 7.16; 24.19. Jesus describes himself as a prophet in Mark 6.4; Luke 4.24; 13.33. The Fourth Gospel also uses this term to describe Jesus in 4.19; 6.14; 7.40; 9.17. Peter and Stephen refer to Jesus as a prophet in Acts 3.22; 7.37.

Matthew's Gospel summarizes Jesus' ministry in a similar way: 'And he went about all Galilee, teaching in their synagogues and preaching the gospel of the kingdom and healing every disease and every infirmity among the people' (4.23; see also 9.35). And in Matthew's Gospel the disciples are also given, as their first priority, the task of seeking the kingdom (6.33), and proclaiming it and working for it (10.7–8).

Luke also emphasizes the kingdom of God as central in the proclamation of Jesus (see 4.43; 8.1; 9.11). In the important opening scene of Jesus' Galilean ministry in Nazareth, as Graham Stanton points out, Luke's presentation stresses how the coming of Jesus marked the fulfilment of the promises of Isaiah 61.1–2. Even though 'the word "kingdom" is not used . . . many of the main points of this passage are related to "kingdom" sayings which Luke includes elsewhere' (Stanton 1989, pp. 189–90).

Hooker, in *The Signs of a Prophet: The Prophetic Actions of Jesus* (1997) shows that the symbolic actions were an integral part of Jesus' identity as a prophet. For the vast majority of times that he was called a prophet – Mark 6.4, 15 and parallels; 8.28 and parallels; Matt. 21.11; Luke 4.24; 7.16 and 24.19; John 6.14 and 9.17 – refer to or are juxtaposed with accounts of what Jesus did. Jesus was regarded as a prophet, not simply because he spoke like a prophet, but because he acted like a prophet (Hooker 1997, p. 16).

Other recent scholarship has supported this view of Jesus (see Powell 1999, for an informative introduction to the whole field). One example is the historian E. P. Sanders, who concludes his penetrating study of the Gospel evidence by describing Jesus as a prophet of the end-time:

> Jesus saw himself as God's last messenger before the establishment of the kingdom. He looked for a new order, created by a mighty act of God. In the new order the twelve tribes would be reassembled, there would be a new temple, force of arms would not be needed, divorce would be neither necessary nor permitted, outcasts – even the wicked – would have a place, and Jesus and his disciples - the poor, the meek, and lowly – would have the leading role. (Sanders, quoted in Powell 1999, p. 123)

Another well-known example is N. T. Wright (1996), who surveys the historical evidence surrounding Jesus' ministry and draws the following conclusions:

> How then was Jesus perceived by the villagers who saw and heard him? All the evidence so far displayed suggests that he was perceived as a *prophet*. His speech and action evoked, even while they went beyond, contemporary pictures of prophetic activity. Furthermore we must conclude that Jesus was conscious of a *vocation* to be a prophet . . . it is possible to explain a good deal of his career, not least its dramatic conclusion, from this basis. (Wright 1996, pp. 196–7)

Wright also shows how Jesus' messiahship and his message about the inauguration of the kingdom of God were part of this prophetic vocation:

> Jesus saw himself as a prophet announcing and inaugurating the kingdom of YHWH; he believed himself to be Israel's true Messiah; he believed that the kingdom would be brought about by means of his own death at the hands of the pagans. (1996, p. 612)

This conclusion is important for our purposes because it allows us to clarify the type of role Jesus called his followers to continue after the resurrection. It is, as argued, the role of a prophet, one who 'forth tells' God's purposes for the world in word and action and who calls on people to respond in their hearts and lives. This is not to deny that he was also Messiah and Son of God but these were not roles that could be passed on to the disciples: they describe what was unique about Jesus, rather than what was transferable to others. A different title, the one most commonly used by others of him in his own day and the one scholarship today uses to sum up the generic character of what he was doing, is that of prophet. If we are to characterize the kind of ministry Jesus lived and bequeathed to his followers, it is that of prophecy.

Mission principles

Mark 1.14–45 also reveals a number of other practical principles within Jesus' Galilean ministry:

1. His mission arises out of the 40 days of fasting in the wilderness, which was a time of listening to the silence, to his own thought and temptations, to Scripture and to his Father. He returns to such places at various subsequent points (e.g. 1.35). Also it is noticeable how, more often than not, he listens to those who come to him with their needs and requests and pays close attention to what they say (e.g. 1.30–1). *Contemplative listening* therefore frames the action of his ministry and is a key part of all that follows.

2. The manner in which Jesus moves around Galilee is significant. There is no mention of any retinue or court following, let alone security guards or militia or army. He comes simply as a wandering preacher, in the clothes he is wearing, at the mercy of the people he is addressing. This shows he was *vulnerable* – he comes with no wealth or status or arms. He is powerless, relying simply on the message he is preaching. (This vulnerability would later have drastic consequences for Jesus, showing how profound it was.)

3. Jesus calls a band of helpers – the disciples – to live, work and assist him in proclaiming the kingdom of God (Mark 1.16–20; see also 3.14). He is not undertaking this ministry on his own but in a dedicated community of men (and women, according to Luke) who share the burden and support each other (as well as have their disagreements). Furthermore he calls both the kind of fisher-

man who do not have boats and must cast their nets, and the wealthier kind who not only have boats but hired servants as well. He even calls an outcast tax collector (2.14). It is clear from these invitations that a shared or *collaborative* type of ministry is to be fundamental to the whole enterprise.

4. Jesus goes to where people are, where they live, work and gather for worship in their synagogues (1.21, 38–9). He does not wait for them to come to him. He becomes immersed in their life, speaking their language, and talking to them at the time of the week, on the Sabbath, when they will give him a hearing. The fact that they do give him a hearing shows that he has gained their respect as one of their own with the right to address their community. He even follows the custom of requiring a cleansed leper to go to the priest for verification (1.44). This shows the principle of identification with the community and that his ministry was locally rooted or *incarnational*.

5. The proclamation of the kingdom involves not just preaching and teaching, but surprising and powerful signs as well, in this case the exorcism of a possessed man in the synagogue at Capernaum (1.21–8). Words are combined with unexpected actions to show that the reign of God is breaking into people's lives. So the proclamation of the kingdom is through signs that help to effect what they are pointing to. In different language it can be said that his proclamation is *sacramental*, where a sacrament is defined as an 'effective sign' (as in Article 25 of the Articles of Religion in the *The Book of Common Prayer* of the Church of England, for example).

6. But who initiates the powerful signs? It is important to note that Jesus does not approach the possessed man but the other way round (1.23): Jesus is almost forced to release him from the possession. So this powerful and saving sign is not planned or sought out by Jesus – it just seems to happen when another comes to him with their need. This happens time after time during the Galilean mission: it is the principle of *surprise*. While his own imperative is to get around as many villages as possible with the message about the kingdom of God (1.38–9), unexpected and wonderful things start to happen within this mission, which he then accepts and works with.

7. At many points Jesus seeks to stop news of the spectacular aspect of his work spreading beyond his followers. He tells those he heals not to publicize the great

healings but to keep quiet (1.25, 34, 44). He openly proclaims the kingdom but also tries to suppress the spread of news about the miraculous ways that that arrival is taking place. This shows a principle of *secrecy* about the spectacular at work in his mission. The interpretation of this feature of his ministry has been debated extensively among scholars and it is not possible here to open up that debate again: only to note that there is a determined attempt by Jesus to keep the focus of his mission on the proclamation of the kingdom rather than on the mighty acts taking place through him.

8. The releasing from possession is not the only sign that takes place. These verses show that all manner of different kinds of healing and release take place through Jesus: the cure of a fever, healing of 'various diseases', making a leper clean, raising a paralytic to his feet (e.g. Mark 1.29–34). Jesus seems to respond to different needs in different kinds of ways, bringing whatever type of healing is most appropriate. His is a multiple or varied kind of ministry which addresses many kinds of physical and mental need. It is, in other words, *all-inclusive*: every kind of ailment from every kind of person is included within its scope. This is confirmed in Matthew's Gospel where Jesus, referring to his own ministry, tells John's disciples to 'Go and tell John what you hear and see: the blind receive their sight and the lame walk, lepers are cleansed and the deaf hear, and the dead are raised up, and the poor have good news preached to them' (Matt. 11.4–5). (Bosch especially emphasizes the all-inclusive nature of Jesus' mission: see Bosch 1991, pp. 28–9.)

9. One further dimension of Jesus' mission in Mark 1 comes to the fore in his healing of the possessed man (and later in the Gospel in his conflict with the Pharisees). It is a *political* agenda of challenging and seeking to re-form the corporate relationships of the Jewish community. Ched Myers has drawn attention to the way Mark's Gospel highlights this:

> The demon in the synagogue becomes the representative of the scribal establishment, whose 'authority' undergirds the dominant Jewish social order. Exorcism represents an act of confrontation in the war of myths in which Jesus asserts his alternative authority. Only this interpretation can explain why exorcism is at issue in the scribal counterattack upon Jesus later in 3.22ff. (Myers 1988, p. 143)

John Dominic Crossan has also drawn attention to this political dimension, especially laying emphasis on the ways Jesus was a social revolutionary (see Powell 1999, ch. 5, and references there). Similarly, N. T. Wright points to the political dimension of Jesus' conflict with the Pharisees. As a party within Judaism the Pharisees were working to an agenda of maintaining the separation and distinctiveness of the Jewish nation from the pagan races that surrounded them in Palestine. Through upholding Sabbath codes and purity laws around meals they sought to maintain clear boundaries and avoid gradual assimilation into the pagan gentile world. But for Jesus these practices had become

> a symptom of the problem rather than part of the solution. The kingdom of the one true god was at last coming into being, and it would be characterized not by defensiveness, but by Israel's being the light of the world; not by the angry zeal which would pay the Gentiles back in their own coin . . . but by turning the other cheek and going the second mile . . . the clash between Jesus and his Jewish contemporaries must be seen in terms of *alternative political agendas* generated by *alternative eschatological beliefs and expectations.* Jesus was announcing the kingdom in a way which did not reinforce, but rather called into question, the agenda of revolutionary zeal which dominated the horizon of, especially, the dominant group within Pharisaism. (Wright 1996, pp. 389–90)

Jesus' politics, then, was to be one of changing the way Israel related to the nations around it. He was seeking to transform those relationships from differentiation and exclusion to openness and integration, so that the truth of the dawning kingdom would become more and more widely known. Jesus was 'offering an alternative construal of Israel's destiny and god-given vocation, an alternative way of telling Israel's true story, and an alternative to the piety which expressed itself in nationalistic symbols' (Wright 1996, p. 390).

Three players

Mark's overview of Jesus' mission in his first chapter therefore shows an unfolding drama with three main players. The first player is the society in which Jesus' ministry takes place. This is the *Jewish society* of Galilee, from which

Jesus comes and to which he addresses his ministry. He does not seek to remove himself from this society, like the Essene sect at Qumran, but seeks to change the consciousness of everyone within it. And because the whole society is addressed, the marginalized and excluded are especially included. The inclusiveness of his ministry will later be symbolized by his choosing of twelve disciples, representing the twelve tribes of Israel and signifying that what he was bringing was for *everyone* within his society.

The second player is the *kingdom of God*, the incoming divine reign that is going to change everything. The full arrival of this kingdom is still awaited, but there are instances of its saving transformation already appearing among the needy and repentant. Its arrival has begun and this provides a powerful sense of urgency to what Jesus is doing.

The third player is *Jesus and his followers* who point to the inauguration of God's kingdom (the macro dimension) and call for a response to this in the hearts and lives of all the people (the micro dimension). It is a ministry that is not primarily about creating a sub-culture within the wider Jewish society of his day, but of working to change the consciousness of everyone within that wider society. Jesus does not do this through force and coercion but through being vulnerable; he does not work alone but includes others within a collaborative ministry; he does not wait for the people to come to him but goes to them, to where they live and work, and so becomes locally identified and rooted; he does not just preach but finds surprising symbolic actions taking place, actions which show the saving reality of the kingdom breaking into people's lives; he does not seek to be sensationalist and is secretive about the wonders, keeping a low profile on occasions; he addresses the actual needs people have, and includes the marginalized and excluded in this ministry, pointing to the holistic liberation of the kingdom. Finally, he incorporates periods of retreat, listening and contemplation for his followers and himself within this mission.

Some Galilean principles

If, as John 20.21 makes clear, Jesus' followers are called to continue his mission, what does all of this imply for the Church?

It shows that the Church is only one among three players, the other two being the society in which it lives, and the coming kingdom of God, which is the participative and saving movement of the Trinitarian God within the world. The Church must always see its place and role within this wider drama: it does not exist to serve its own ends but has been formed *to point to* the inauguration of that kingdom within that society. This is a prophetic role expressed through word and deed. It is one that calls for a response in the hearts and lives of the people of that society, and will result in surprising instances of the kingdom's saving presence in those lives. It is not, then, primarily concerned with creating a special society within the wider society of the day, but has a vocation of working to assist the transformation of everyone within that wider society.

The Church is therefore called to a kind of diaconal activity, of being an ambassador for the coming of the kingdom, rather than of being a static institution that exists to serve its own life. (See Clark 2005, for an exploration of the diaconal dimension of the life of the Church.)

This prophetic role continues the mission of Christ. Based on exegesis of Mark 1 with its overview of Jesus' Galilean ministry, and drawing on the insights of contemporary biblical scholarship, we can deduce that it will embody the following principles of interaction with others, principles that can be used to assess subsequent developments in mission:

- *Contemplative listening*, which frames Jesus' ministry: listening to God, to other people, to himself, especially in times of prayer and retreat.
- *Addressing society as a whole*, at points where people live and work, including and especially the marginalized. This results in being received and accepted by some but rejected and opposed by others.
- *Pointing to the inaugurated yet still awaited kingdom*, in word and in surprising saving deed (symbolic actions) which address the actual needs of people (both individual and structural); but without publicizing the wonders.
- *Calling for a personal response* to the coming of this kingdom by those who hear and see what he is doing.
- Doing all this through *a collaborative team*, who themselves are powerless and vulnerable and must suffer the consequences.

Taken together, these principles show that mission encompasses every aspect of who Jesus' followers are as well as all that they do: it encompasses their *being* as well as their *doing*. In other words the principles show that Christian mission can no longer be seen as one discrete aspect of church life alongside others such as worship or pastoral care. Christian mission will encompass the whole way the Church lives out its life in society, including its internal life as well as its outreach. Its congregational worship, music, social life, administration, stewardship of buildings, and at a deeper level its spirituality, are all part of mission. At a wider level the whole network of ways it relates to its surroundings, formally and informally, is part of the picture. It will also include the whole difference the Church makes to the community and society in which it exists. This is not just a sociological question about things that can be measured and quantified, such as attendance or giving, but is an ethnographic question about the difference a church makes to the lives of the people it touches within the complex web of relationships within a community (see Jenkins 1999, for illuminating explorations of this dimension).

But this introduces a further dimension, for communities and cultures do not stand still but are continually evolving and developing through time, sometimes in dramatic ways. They are formed by shifting currents of social and cultural change, so that the way the Church participates in mission in one culture and at one time will need to be different from the way it participates in mission in another culture at a different time.

The five Galilean principles provide general guidance about the nature of this participation but they do not provide detailed guidance about its expression within different cultures and regions, among people of different languages and customs and peculiarities. For that kind of guidance it is necessary to visit the currents and cross-currents of human history, where Church, culture and kingdom interact in different ways at different times. Through the study of this changing interrelationship it will be possible to get to know the specific ways the Christian community has participated and does participate in the *missio Dei*. As Bosch writes,

> the Christian faith is a *historical* faith. God communicates his revelation to people through human beings and through events, not by means of abstract propositions. This is another way of saying that the biblical faith, both Old and New Testament, is 'incarnational', the reality of God entering human affairs. (Bosch 1991, p. 181)

The study of the history of this participation and communication is the subject of the next and central section of this *Studyguide*.

Discussion questions

Are there other important mission principles within Jesus' Galilean ministry?
In what order would you place them and why?
Which episodes from the Gospels especially exemplify them?

Further reading

Bauckham, Richard (2003), *Bible and Mission: Christian Witness in a Postmodern World*, Paternoster

Bosch, David J. (1991), *Transforming Mission: Paradigm Shifts in Theology of Mission*, Orbis

Brueggemann, Walter (2001), *The Prophetic Imagination*, 2nd edition, Fortress Press

Clark, David (2005), *Breaking the Mould of Christendom: Kingdom Community, Diaconal Church and the Liberation of the Laity*, SCM Press

Gillingham, S. E. (1998), *One Bible, Many Voices*, SPCK

Hooker, Morna D. (1991), *The Gospel according to St Mark*, A & C Black

Hooker, Morna D. (1997), *The Signs of a Prophet: The Prophetic Actions of Jesus*, SCM Press

Jenkins, Timothy (1999), *Religion in English Everyday Life*, Berghahn

Knitter, Paul (1996), *Jesus and the Other Names: Christian Mission and Global Responsibility*, Orbis

Myers, C. (1988), *Binding the Strong Man: A Political Reading of Mark's Story of Jesus*, Orbis

Powell, Mark Allan (1999), *The Jesus Debate: Modern Historians Investigate the Life of Christ*, Lion

Senior, D., and C. Stuhlmueller (1983), *The Biblical Foundation of Mission*, Orbis

Stanton, Graham (1989), *The Gospels and Jesus*, Oxford University Press

Wright, N. T. (1996), *Jesus and the Victory of God*, SPCK

Part 2

Types and Expressions

World is crazier and more of it than we think,
Incorrigibly plural. I peel and portion
A tangerine and spit the pips and feel
The drunkenness of things being various

(Louis MacNeice, 'Snow')

Introduction

Christian history presents a confusing interchange of movements, people and ideas: on the one hand, the great institutions of Christendom, such as the papacy, the Orthodox patriarchates and the European monarchies stand over and dominate that history at many points; on the other hand, the mavericks and mystics of the Christian tradition, such as Antony of Egypt, Francis of Assisi and Julian of Norwich, show a completely different, subversive and equally influential side to the story. When we ask, as we must now do, how Christian mission has been expressed over the centuries we are therefore asking a question that cannot be answered in a simple and straightforward way. It is a question about the whole complex and involved way the Christian tradition has developed through its institutions, people and ideas and also through its encounter with different cultures and contexts. Christian history bears ample witness to the truth of Louis MacNeice's verse of 'things being various'. Clearly some sifting and summarizing of that history is going to be necessary.

To begin to do this we can recall a conclusion from the last section, that the Church is only one among three players, as it were, the others being the social and cultural world in which it lives, and the inaugurated kingdom of God (which was defined as the participative and saving movement of the Trinitarian God within that world). When looking at Christian history it will therefore be important to trace the ways in which the Church has related to these other two players. This is the crucial three-way relationship which determines the essential nature of mission.

In the following survey, then, the point will not be to describe the history of Christian mission in chronological order with every key personality and movement given space in the narrative (see Neill 1964, Comby 1996, and Yates 2004 for comprehensive and accessible examples of this approach). Instead it will be to uncover the changing relationship between the three players of world, kingdom and Church. It will be to identify different stages in that relationship and examine each in turn even though some were more short-lived than others. Well-known figures and movements will need to be mentioned in so far as they contributed to the development of that relationship, but not otherwise. So, for example, Martin Luther will need to figure prominently, because he was instrumental in breaking the close identification of church and kingdom in late medieval Catholicism. Under his influence many came to see a profound distinction between the visible Church, which belonged among the kingdoms of this world, and God's kingdom, which somehow transcended this world, and this distinction fundamentally changed the nature of mission. John Calvin, on the other hand, while very influential as a theologian, inherited Luther's thinking on this point and mostly worked within it: for this reason he will not need to receive equal attention.

Hans Küng has provided a comprehensive and widely used overview of the terrain, employing a theory of paradigms and paradigm shifts as an interpretative tool. In the following chapters his paradigms will be employed, with each one introduced and explained and, with the help of David J. Bosch, their different approaches to mission drawn out. Also as the discussion proceeds each approach will be compared with the mission of Christ (as described above), seeing how far it embodied the Galilean principles, so that it can be compared and assessed for use within mission today.

Paradigms and paradigm shifts in the history of Christianity

Thomas S. Kuhn, in *The Structure of Scientific Revolutions* (2nd edn 1970) classically defined a paradigm as 'an entire constellation of beliefs, values, techniques, and so on, shared by the members of a given community. It is an entire world-view.' N. T. Wright elucidates this in a helpful way: 'Worldviews are the lenses through which a society looks at the world, the grid upon which are plotted the multiple experiences of life.' He continues by saying that world-views may be studied through certain features such as 'characteristic stories; fundamental symbols; habitual praxis; and a set of questions and answers (who are

we? where are we? what's wrong? what's the solution? and what time is it?)'
(Wright 1996, p. 138).

A *paradigm shift* takes place when there is a leap from one world-view to
another which allows the world to be explained and interpreted in a whole
new way. A powerful example was the Copernican revolution, when Nicholas
Copernicus (1473–1543) established that the universe did not revolve around
the earth (with humankind at its centre), as in Greek astronomy, but that the
earth revolved around the sun. Humankind was no longer at the centre of
things, in an ordered and static world: the universe was altogether a larger and
more mysterious thing, with humanity on a ball of rock floating around within
it. It became something that more than ever called out for investigation.

Even though Copernicus dedicated his book to the Pope, its theory was so
unsettling that it was placed on the index of forbidden works. But a rubicon had
been crossed: in the West a shift began to take place in the way we view ourselves and our world, a paradigm shift from an ancient to a modern outlook.

Kuhn mentions another example, the shift from a Newtonian picture of the
world (which talks about particles and forces and positions and times) to the
world of quantum theory (which talks about probabilities, measurements, mix-
tures of particles and waves) and relativity theory (where there is no fixed space
or time). Such a shift of understanding was revolutionary and brought about
a whole new way of seeing our place in the universe, one that has often been
described as 'relativism'.

In 1984 David Tracy and Hans Küng adopted the use of the idea of paradigm shifts to explain the evolving nature of the Church's theology and self-
understanding over the centuries (see *Paradigm Shifts in Theology*, 1984, English
trans. T & T Clark, 1989). In Küng's voluminous book of 1994, *Christianity: Its
Essence and History* (English trans. 1995), he put this theory to work by map-
ping out Christian history and theology into six basic periods, each with its
own paradigm. The movement from one to the next was a revolutionary jump
in the whole 'world-view' or theological system of the Christian community, a
paradigm shift for the Church. (See Walls 1996, ch. 2, for a similar and concise
overview of Christian history which gives greater recognition to the role of cultures in changing paradigms.)

At the start of his book Küng provided an illuminating diagrammatic summary of what was to follow, and this is reproduced in an amended form as a reference point for our own survey. The diagram makes a number of key points:

Paradigm shifts in Christianity

Adapted from Hans Küng, *Christianity: Its Essence and History*, 1995

Defining events and people

Ist century
Jewish
Christianity
in Palestine
Peter, Paul
Persecutions

2nd–5th century
Gnosticism
Origen, Athanasius
Cappadocians
Antony of Egypt
Emperor Constantine
Nicaea, Chalcedon
Celtic Christianity
Augustine of Hippo

6th–15th century
Gregory I
Augustine of Canterbury
Charlemagne
Medieval popes
incl. Gregory VII
Crusades
Mendicant orders
Aquinas & scholasticism

16th–18th century
Luther and Reformation
Zwingli and Calvin
Tyndale and Cranmer
Anabaptists
Wars of religion
Pietists
Wesley, Whitfield and evangelical
revivals

18th–20th century
Locke, Paley, Kant
Missionary education
and medical work
Schleiermacher, Hegel
Biblical criticism
F. D. Maurice to W. Temple
Ecumenical movement
Vatican II, Rahner

20th–21st century
Barth and crisis theology
Bonhoeffer
Interfaith dialogue
contextual theology, e.g.
feminist, Asian, African
Emerging church movement

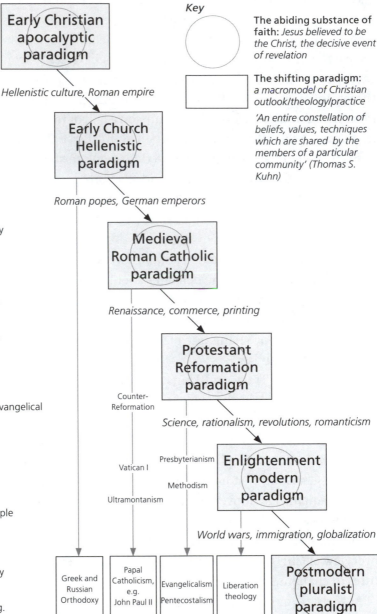

Figure 1

(a) While there was continuity of faith in Jesus as Lord and saviour over the centuries (the dotted circle that appears in each box), the intellectual framework that held this belief in place changed from one era to the next (the square boxes that run down the page).

(b) Each of the paradigms has continued to be expressed in subsequent periods and can be found in different parts of the Christian world today. The faint lines and boxes that run to the bottom of the page represent this. The Hellenistic paradigm, for example, is still dominant within Greek Orthodox traditionalism in many parts of Eastern Europe.

(c) New paradigms have come about as a result of social, political and cultural influences (the italicized words in between the boxes) as well as the influence of certain theologians and church leaders (the people listed down the left hand side of the boxes). This shows the creative interaction of the Christian tradition with different cultures through history: it shows how Christianity has been translated from one cultural setting to another in sometimes surprising and radical ways through different eras.

Mission within the paradigms

In *Transforming Mission: Paradigm Shifts in the Theology of Mission* (1991), Bosch used Küng's framework as the basis of his own survey of the history of Christian mission, employing it to make sense of the different ways mission has been understood and practised. Bosch draws on the views of key theologians, official church pronouncements and the ways missionary work was carried out, to present concise and perceptive portraits of mission in different eras. While he does not cover every period with equal thoroughness his book gives what is generally regarded as the most comprehensive overview to be published in the last two decades. (See *Transforming Mission*, pp. 181–9 for a full explanation of his approach.)

A recent book by Stephen B. Bevans and Roger P. Schroeder, *Constants in Context: A Theology of Mission for Today* (2004) must also be mentioned. This supplements Bosch's book with extensive treatment of movements and missionaries not described by Bosch, especially within Roman Catholic mission around the world from the Middle Ages to the modern era. It is a mine of information and insight and complements the Protestant emphasis of Bosch's book.

(See also Yates 1994 for a more detailed presentation of twentieth-century mission theology.)

Building on Bosch's presentation, though, we can go one stage further and isolate the distinctive *type* of mission found within each paradigm. The category of 'type', as mentioned on p. vii of this book, was first used of religious subjects by Max Weber and Ernst Troeltsch. A type is a genuine if stylized representation of an authentic theological tradition (Graham, Walton and Ward 2005, p. 11). At the start of the twentieth century, as we saw, Troeltsch developed what has become a classic typology of religious organizations with his distinction between a 'church' type and 'sect' type. Other writers, mostly notably H. Richard Niebuhr, have adopted and developed this approach. Niebuhr presented five types of relationship between Christianity and wider culture (Niebuhr 1951). Most recently, Elaine Graham, Heather Walton and Frances Ward have analysed and described different forms of theological reflection by employing their own helpful typology (Graham, Walton and Ward 2005, especially pp. 11–12). This book seeks to do the same for mission. Within each paradigm it identifies the distinctive feature of its mission, a feature that sums up the way in which the outreach of the institutional Church or individual Christians related to the other two key 'players' of (first) the social and cultural world in which it lived and (second) the coming kingdom of God. The chapters do this through comparing each paradigm with the others and identifying a phrase, such as 'establishing Christendom' or 'building the kingdom on earth', which employs key missional concepts from that paradigm in an epigrammatic way. Using the historical overviews of Küng and Bosch, then, the following chapters identify six such types of mission, types which have influenced the practice of mission down the centuries. This will enable us to locate contemporary practices in relation to the received traditions of the paradigms.

It should be added that the choice of examples for each type, examples which are indicative and exemplary of their development, reflects the Western provenance of this book. It is written within a Western setting for a mainly Western audience. If it was being written within the global South the choice of examples would to some extent be different. Also, in the same way that the book is not a survey of mission history neither is it a presentation of all mission theology. Bosch attempted to provide such a survey, especially in his presentation of twentieth-century mission theology in the massive penultimate chapter of *Transforming Mission* (which he optimistically entitled 'The emerging ecumenical missionary paradigm'). This *Studyguide* does not attempt to do the same thing: instead it concentrates on six fundamental types and expressions of mission, believing that these lie behind much of that mission history and theology.

Discussion questions

Are there some significant omissions from Küng's list of paradigms (Figure 1)?
What are the weaknesses of this kind of way of gaining an overview of Christian history, and what are its strengths?

Further reading

Bevans, Stephen B., and Roger P. Schroeder (2004), *Constants in Context: A Theology of Mission for Today*, Orbis

Bosch, David J. (1991), *Transforming Mission: Paradigm Shifts in the Theology of Mission*, Orbis.

Comby, Jean (1996), *How to Understand the History of Christian Mission*, SCM Press

Graham, Elaine, Heather Walton and Frances Ward (2005), *Theological Reflection: Methods*, SCM Press

Kuhn, Thomas S. (1970), *The Structure of Scientific Revolutions*, 2nd edn, University of Chicago Press

Küng, Hans (1995), *Christianity: Its Essence and History*, SCM Press

Küng, Hans, and David Tracy, eds. (1989), *Paradigm Shifts in Theology*, T & T Clark

Neill, Stephen (1964), *A History of Christian Missions*, Penguin

Niebuhr, H. Richard (1951), *Christ and Culture*, Harper & Row

Walls, Andrew F. (1996), *The Missionary Movement in Christian History: Studies in the Transmission of Faith*, Orbis

Wright, N. T. (1996), *Jesus and the Victory of God*, SPCK

Yates, Timothy (1994), *Christian Mission in the Twentieth Century*, Cambridge University Press

Yates, Timothy (2004), *The Expansion of Christianity*, Lion

5

Filling the Ark
Apostolic Mission

There is a fresco from third-century Carthage in which the church is pictured as Noah's ark, riding the waves of destruction. A dove is shown flying from the ark in search of land (Frend 1984, p. 337). It is a simple but powerful image, suggesting that the Church is a place of safety and security which is able to ride the waves of lawlessness and chaos engulfing the world outside. It encourages believers to seek out and then find safety within the confines of the Christian community, only going out to rescue others by bringing them into its protective custody. Such an image does not encourage the Church to try to change the wider society, only to rescue individuals out of its swirling waters before the end.

Such an image is a stylized representation of a certain approach to mission, an approach that has its origins in certain texts from the earliest period of the Church's life. To understand this approach, the first of the six historic types located within the Christian paradigms identified by Küng and Bosch, it is necessary to understand the underlying world-view of the first Christians.

Background: Jewish Christianity (c.40–100 AD)

The first Christians were Jews. They came to faith within the Jewish world-view of the time. For many Palestinian Jews this was a world-view dominated by eschatology: they believed the end of the age was near, a time of war, destruction and catastrophe with a promise of salvation for the people of Israel. For many the book of Daniel summed up what they believed: 'At the time of the end . . . there shall be a time of anguish, such as has never occurred since nations first came into existence.' (Daniel 11.40–12.1) There would be deliverance for the people of Israel in these end-times:

> But at that time your people shall be delivered, everyone who is found written in the book. Many of those who sleep in the dust of the earth shall awake, some to everlasting life, and some to shame and everlasting contempt. Those who are wise shall shine like the brightness of the sky, and those who lead many to righteousness, like the stars for ever and ever. (12.1–3)

Many Palestinian Jews at the time of Jesus interpreted these and other similar passages from non-canonical apocalyptic literature as a description of how Roman oppression would be thrown off and a new age of liberation and prosperity begin for the people of Israel. They expected this ending of the age to take place very soon (Figure 2).

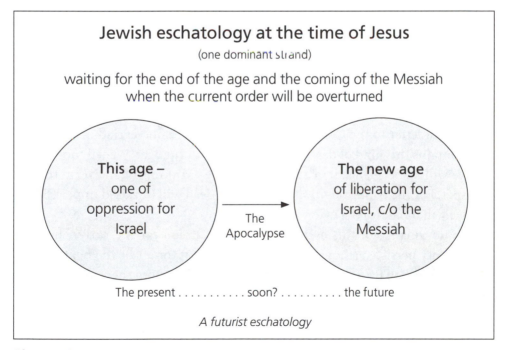

Figure 2

The disciples had been brought up within this world-view and after the resurrection came to believe that Jesus was the figure described in an earlier chapter of the book of Daniel: 'I saw one like a son of man coming with the clouds of heaven' (Daniel 7.13). They believed that Jesus was the long awaited messiah, the Christ. They came to see that his life, death and resurrection were the inauguration of the end-times and that he would soon return in power 'to deliver us from the present evil age' (Galatians 1.4). They believed that he would return within their own lifetimes to do this. Paul's first letter to the Thessalonians, generally recognized as the earliest book in the New Testament, probably written in the early 50s of the first century, provides one of the most vivid examples of this Christian reinterpretation of Jewish eschatological beliefs:

> we who are alive, who are left until the coming of the Lord, will by no means precede those who have died. For the Lord himself, with a cry of command, with the archangel's call and with the sound of God's trumpet, will descend from heaven, and the dead in Christ will rise first. Then we who are alive, who are left, will be caught up in the clouds together with them to meet the Lord in the air; and so we shall be with the Lord for ever. (1 Thess. 4.15–17)

The connection to the book of Daniel is clear: the same kind of language is being used to describe what is going to happen. But now a messiah and the people he is going to save are identified within this picture of the end-times: the messiah is Jesus Christ, and the people he will save are those who believe in him, Gentiles as well as Jews.

The first letter to the Corinthians, written in the same period of Paul's life, also contains this kind of description of the end of the age: 'We will not all die, but we will all be changed, in a moment, in the twinkling of an eye, at the last trumpet. For the trumpet will sound, and the dead will be raised imperishable, and we will be changed' (1 Cor. 15.51–2).

The dominance of this eschatological expectation for the early Christian community persisted (though it was not dominant for all, as the next chapter will show). When Paul wrote his letter to the church in Rome he reminded them 'what time it is, how it is now the moment for you to wake from sleep. For salvation is nearer to us now than when we became believers; the night is far gone, the day is near' (Rom. 13.11–12).

It was still dominant a decade or two later, when the first of the Gospels came to be written, probably that of Mark in the late 60s or early 70s. It is seen in the way the Gospel summarizes the message of Jesus, with his words 'The time is fulfilled, and the kingdom of God has come near' placed at the head of the account of his ministry (1.15). It is also seen in the style of the Gospel, which moves the action forward in a swift and urgent way, using the phrase 'and immediately' many times through the text, creating a sense of breathlessness within the narrative. It is also seen in the positioning of one of Jesus' most specific statements about the coming of the end at the centre and turning point of the Gospel. This is the statement in 9.1 that there were some of his followers who would not die before they saw the kingdom of God come with power. This saying is placed in a key pivotal position, between Jesus' early Galilean ministry and his journey to Jerusalem and suffering and death. And then, most telling of all, the last time Jesus teaches his followers before his arrest he talks about the apocalypse: he describes the end of the age, widespread destruction and his own return, when he would come 'in clouds with great power and glory' (13.1–37, esp. v. 26). The allusions to the book of Daniel and other Jewish apocalyptic literature are again clear, but the reinterpretation of Jewish beliefs about the messiah to refer to himself is even clearer. The layout and content of Mark's Gospel therefore shows that for the second and third generation of Christians the expectation that Christ would soon return at the end of the age was still a dominating belief.

Matthew's Gospel also demonstrates this outlook by placing Jesus' eschatological teaching and parables in the highly significant position immediately preceding the passion narrative (chapters 24–5). Furthermore the very last words of the Gospel remind the reader that the age in which they live will end (28.19).

Another example can be drawn from 1 Peter, which is dominated by the expectation that salvation is about to be revealed 'in the last time' (1.5): 'The end of all things is near' (1 Peter 4.7). All of these passages justify Bosch's statement that 'a high strung expectation of the end characterises the early Christian community' (Bosch 1991, p. 40).

What was it like to live within a world-view that expected an imminent end to the age? 1 Corinthians 7.29–31 gives an evocative portrait of how priorities and allegiances changed:

I mean, brothers and sisters, the appointed time has grown short; from now on, let even those who have wives be as though they had none, and those who mourn as though they were not mourning, and those who rejoice as though they were not rejoicing, and those who buy as though they had no possessions, and those who deal with the world as though they had no dealings with it. For the present form of this world is passing away.

This passage shows how belief in the imminence of the parousia changed everything. The usual customs and routines were no longer relevant: the coming of the messiah put the whole of life in a transitory light. It explains why the first Christians were so willing to sell all their possessions and put the proceeds in a common fund (Acts 2.45; 4.34): an imminent ending of the world demanded a radical response. It also explains why the Church did not seek to change the society in which it lived, for example through seeking to abolish slavery. To modern eyes it is strange and upsetting that the first Christians who espoused the love of neighbour seemed to accept this oppressive institution in Roman society (e.g. 1 Peter 2.18). But when their eschatological world-view is recalled it can be seen that they would not have seen any point in trying to abolish slavery, for every earthly institution and structure would soon be destroyed.

Jewish-Christian apostolic mission

The imminent ending of the age meant that it was desperately important that as many people as possible were told about the offer of salvation and the need to repent. The population of the Roman world needed to be alerted to the fact that the days were short, the end-times were near and destruction was just around the corner. It was imperative that people turn to the Lord, put their lives in order and be made ready for his coming.

Peter's speech on the day of Pentecost (Acts 2.14–42) expresses this approach to mission very well. It is possibly an idealized account of the historical event but it provides the classical example of the apostolic mission type, where Peter frames everything he says within contemporary Jewish eschatological belief: he quotes the prophet Joel's description of the last days and says that this is what is happening now, on this day of Pentecost: "'I will show portents in the heaven above and signs on the earth below, blood, and fire, and smoky mist . . . Then everyone who calls on the name of the Lord shall be saved"' (2.19–21). But contrary to Jewish expectation Peter then argues that the messiah has already come, and he is Jesus of Nazareth: Jesus is the one who is fulfilling the expect-ation of the coming of the messiah in the Scriptures, and so it is he who will shortly reappear with power and glory. Peter then calls on the people to

> 'Repent, and be baptized every one of you in the name of Jesus Christ so that your sins may be forgiven; and you will receive the gift of the Holy Spirit. For the promise is for you, for your children, and for all who are far away, every-one whom the Lord our God calls to him.' (Acts 2.38–9)

Finally, in words that recall the way Noah and his family were separated and saved from 'his generation' (Genesis 6.9), Peter calls on the crowd to 'Save your-selves from this corrupt generation' (Acts 2.40). Peter therefore implies that repentance and baptism is the doorway into a new Noah's ark, the community of Jesus' disciples, which is a place to ride out the coming storm of destruction. Hence this approach to mission can be summed up in the phrase *filling the ark of salvation*. This is a stylized typological description where the Church is the ark that will rescue people from the rising deluge.

Later, in the Temple, Peter's words again show how this approach to mission is intimately bound up with eschatological beliefs about the imminent ending of the age and the parousia of the messiah:

> 'Repent, therefore, and turn to God so that your sins may be wiped out, so that times of refreshing may come from the presence of the Lord, and that he may send the Messiah appointed for you, that is, Jesus, who must remain in heaven until the time of universal restoration that God announced long ago through his holy prophets.' (Acts 3.19–21)

Christian mission, then, was all about appealing to the hearts and minds of Jews, and then of Gentiles, to bring about repentance and belief in Jesus the messiah before it was too late. It was not about changing cultures, general cus-toms or structures, as there was no time to do this. It was about the apostolic Church engaging in a 'search and rescue' operation.

The book of Acts shows Paul adopting and extending this approach in his missionary journeys. In the first of his extended speeches in Acts 13 (vv. 16–41), at the start of his missionary journeys, he argues that Jesus has fulfilled the promises given to David (v. 34) and therefore was the longed-for messiah. Paul announces that 'through this man forgiveness of sins is proclaimed to you; by this Jesus everyone who believes is set free from all those sins from which you could not be freed by the law of Moses' (13.38–9). The focus of mission, then, remains changing the minds and hearts of the Jews (and later the Gentiles) who listen to the apostle. It is not primarily about healing, though some healings do take place, nor is it about attacking Roman oppression, though it questions the deity of the emperor. It is about encouraging the *metanoia* of his audience or, in other words, encouraging them to enter a whole new mind-set centred on the Lordship of Christ. This type of mission is fulfilled primarily through speaking in synagogues and public places, addressing the people through preaching and teaching.

Drawing on the famous writings of Roland Allen, Vincent Donovan has drawn attention to the contrast between Paul's approach to mission and that of the modern Church in Africa and elsewhere. Allen notes that Paul's whole strategy was based on covering a wide area with some speed, spending no longer than two and a half years in one place. He sought to cover each Roman province from just a few centres. When he left one centre he considered his work done (Allen, quoted in Donovan 1982, p. 36). Donovan contrasts this approach with twentieth-century Catholic missionary work in places like Tanzania, an approach which inundated a country with hundreds of priests and religious and built permanent mission stations with schools and clinics every few miles. Donovan sadly noted how few of the Masai had come to faith despite this huge ecclesial presence. The difference between Catholic mission and Paul's mission may be due in part to their different world-views: neither the Masai nor the missionaries thought the world was about to end and so there was no sense of urgency. But it is also due to different mission objectives: for one mission was all about spreading a message, for the other it was all about serving the educational and medical needs of society.

For Paul, as for Peter, the heart of Christian mission was all about alerting as many people as possible to the way Christ could save them from imminent destruction: it was about preparing them and their households for a new age when *everything* would be different.

Case study: Paul's calling

The letters of Paul dominate the second half of the New Testament and have dominated much of the thinking of the Church ever since they were written. They have been used within every era of Christian history to justify the theology and practice of that era. They are complex, involved and sometimes untidy pieces of writing that develop his thinking in many different directions. They are therefore difficult documents to draw upon when studying the life of the early Church. But in certain crucial respects they clearly exemplify the subject of this chapter, the apostolic mission type.

They do this through the way they show Paul defining his own role. It is significant that when he introduces himself he does not describe himself as a church leader, such as a bishop or presbyter, or as a Christian teacher or theologian, or as a social or community worker, roles that at different points in later eras *would* define the heart of missionary work. He uses a different term and explains its meaning by putting it within a wider context of events. It is a term found in the opening of many of his letters, 'apostle'. Galatians provides a good example: 'Paul, an apostle – sent neither by human commission nor from human authorities, but through Jesus Christ and God the Father, who raised him from the dead' (1.1). The word 'apostle' was a common term in the Hellenistic world and simply meant one who is sent as an emissary with a message. So Paul's calling is to be one who is given an official task of handing on the message of another. Later in the letter Paul provides a fuller description of the nature of this role:

For I want you to know, brothers and sisters, that the gospel that was proclaimed by me is not of human origin; for I did not receive it from a human source, nor was I taught it, but I received it through a revelation of Jesus Christ. You have heard, no doubt, of my earlier life in Judaism. I was violently persecuting the church of God and was trying to destroy it. I advanced in Judaism beyond many among my people of the same age, for I was far more zealous for the traditions of my ancestors. But when God, who had set me apart before I was born and called me through his grace, was pleased to reveal his Son to me, so that I might proclaim him among the Gentiles, I did not confer with any human being, nor did I go up to Jerusalem to those who were already apostles before me, but I went away at once into Arabia, and afterwards I returned to Damascus. (1.11–17)

This quotation reveals a number of features of Paul's calling. It shows it was based on an initial powerful experience often called his conversion. In this event there was 'an analysis of reality triggered by an initial experience that gave Paul a new world-view' (Senior and Stuhlmueller 1983, p. 171). It led Paul to believe he was not serving his own plans but was serving someone else, Jesus the messiah, who at the beginning of the epistle was described as having given himself for our sins 'to set us free from the present evil age' (1.3). This, crucially, locates Paul's apostleship within the wider eschatological framework we examined earlier: the end of the age has been inaugurated and the messiah is soon to return and save those who believe in him. Paul's calling is to pass on the news about all of this to others. Second, it shows that God chose Paul before he was born for his apostleship, which demonstrates a divine mission behind all that is taking place. Third, that the specific task for Paul was to proclaim Christ among the Gentiles (unlike the Twelve who were sent to the house of Israel): 'It is his task to name the Messiah where he has not so far been named, rather than building on anyone else's foundation . . . Paul clearly sees himself as a *pioneer*' (Wright 2005, p. 162). Fourth, that this apostleship was an expression of grace: he had been blessed through it.

All that Paul subsequently does, then, in his speaking, work and writing, flows from this calling: his letters and their theology must ultimately be seen as serving this apostolic mission, one that comes out of the great eschatological events that have begun to come to pass.

In 1 Corinthians 15 he confirms how this mission is as much focused on the future as on the past. He begins the passage by describing the gospel that he has been given and which he passes on to others, the gospel through which they are being saved:

> For I handed on to you as of first importance what I in turn had received: that Christ died for our sins in accordance with the scriptures, and that he was buried, and that he was raised on the third day in accordance with the scriptures, and that he appeared to Cephas, then to the twelve . . . Last of all, as to someone untimely born, he appeared also to me. (1 Cor. 15.3–8)

Then, at some length, he describes how resurrection from the dead of those who belong to Christ is integral to this gospel: 'If for this life only we have hoped in Christ, we are of all people most to be pitied' (v. 19). Paul then describes how this resurrection will take place:

for as all die in Adam, so all will be made alive in Christ. But each in his own order: Christ the first fruits, then at his coming those who belong to Christ. Then comes the end, when he hands over the kingdom to God the Father, after he has destroyed every ruler and every authority and power. For he must reign until he has put all his enemies under his feet. The last enemy to be destroyed is death. (1 Cor. 15.22–6)

Paul is showing that Jewish eschatological expectations and hopes were to be fulfilled by Christ's return, but not in quite the way the Judaism of his day was expecting. When Christ returned he would raise those 'who belong' to him. Paul is implying, like Peter in the book of Acts, that the Church is a kind of ark that will save those within it from the coming deluge.

It is imperative, then, that he reaches as many as possible and proclaims deliverance 'from the wrath that is coming' (1 Thess. 1.10). His own apostolic mission is directed toward this salvation at the parousia. Under the expectation of Christ's imminent return, mission was to be the gathering of the elect into the eschatological community of the Church, the ark of salvation, and this was quite simply the overriding concern.

N. T. Wright expands and refines this eschatological view of Paul in his recent *Paul: Fresh Perspectives* (2005), drawing in other key themes of his theology:

Paul, then, held what we might call a covenantal and apocalyptic theology in which, in surprising fulfilment of the covenant, God has unveiled his plan, his character, and not least his saving, restorative justice through the events concerning Jesus the Messiah, and would complete this revelation once and for all at Jesus' final appearing, his eventual royal presence. And this means, as is well known, that his theology has the character of *inaugurated eschatology*, that is, of a sense that God's ultimate future has come forwards into the middle of history, so that the church is living within – indeed, is constituted precisely by living simultaneously within! – God's new world and the present one. The age to come has already arrived with Jesus; but it will be consummated in the future. The church must order its life and witness, its holiness and love, along that axis. (Wright 2005, p. 57)

This eschatology, ecclesiology and missiology are represented in Figure 3, which also shows how Paul and the apostolic Church adapted the Jewish eschatological ideas represented in Figure 2.

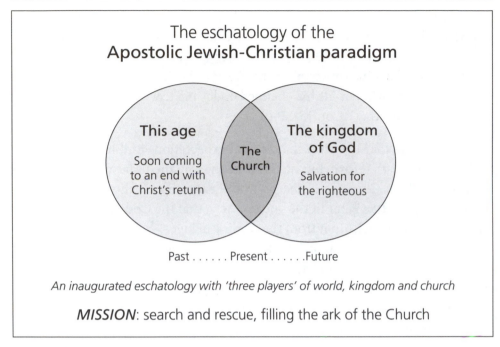

The eschatology of the
Apostolic Jewish-Christian paradigm

This age

Soon coming
to an end with
Christ's return

The Church

The kingdom of God

Salvation for
the righteous

Past . . . . . . Present . . . . . .Future

An inaugurated eschatology with 'three players' of world, kingdom and church

MISSION: search and rescue, filling the ark of the Church

Figure 3

Some more recent expressions of the type

One of the key features of Küng's paradigm theory is that each paradigm is not just located at a distant point in the past but lives on, through the traditions of certain Christian communities, in the modern era. Each paradigm represents the outlook of parts of the Church today, who have continued to live and worship and do their theology within its parameters.

The Anabaptists

One example comes from the Anabaptist movement which has its roots in the German Reformation of the sixteenth century and has been expressed in radical Baptist traditions such as those of the Amish, the Brethren and the Mennonites, often with a strong apocalyptic flavour.

A foundational belief of Anabaptism was the conviction that the Christian life only truly begins with a conscious and informed commitment to Christ, and therefore can only take place when a child becomes a young adult. This means that baptism should be reserved to adults, and anyone baptized as a child needs to be re-baptized as an adult (hence their name *Anabaptists*, which is derived from the Greek for 're-baptizer'). Anabaptists were very critical of the Lutheran and Reformed traditions which allowed infant baptism and this led them to develop an understanding of their fellowship as the one true Church, a voluntary association of adults who had experienced conversion. They saw the Church as a covenant fellowship, devoted to a disciplined life among its members on a path of obedient discipleship, holy living and suffering in the spirit of Christ. Membership of the Church was therefore a 'bounded-set', one that 'has clear boundaries and maintains the integrity of the community by excluding any whose beliefs or behaviour are unacceptable' (Murray 2004b, p. 27). It was, in other words, to be an ark of the faithful in a sea of corruption and degradation.

This was seen in their attitude to any of their number who fell into scandal and refused to repent. Balthasar Hubmaier (?1485–1528), one of the leading German Anabaptists, evocatively described what was involved in an early Reformation context:

> It is exclusion and separation to such an extent that no fellowship is held with such a person by Christians, whether in speaking, eating, drinking, grinding, baking, or in any other way, but he is treated as a heathen and a publican, who is bound and delivered over to Satan. He is to be avoided and shunned, lest the entire visible church be evil spoken of, disgraced and dishonoured by his company, and corrupted by his example, instead of being startled and made afraid by his punishment, so that they will mortify their sins. (in Little 2000, p. 88)

Vatican I

Exclusive understandings of the Church have not been limited to Protestant traditions. Pius IX (pope from 1846 to 1878), the liberal turned conservative defender of the papacy against its loss of political power in nineteenth-century Europe, explicitly referred to the Church as an ark of salvation, though he qualified this with some reticence about saying whether only those within this ark would be saved:

> We must hold as of the faith, that outside of the Apostolic Roman Church there is no salvation; that she is the only ark of safety, and whosoever is not in her perishes in the deluge; we must also, on the other hand, recognize with certainty that those who are invincible in ignorance of the true religion are not guilty for this in the eyes of the Lord. And who would presume to mark out the limits of this ignorance according to the character and diversity of peoples, countries, minds and the rest? (Pius IX, 9 December 1854)

This model of the Church found its way into some of the documents of the First Vatican Council of 1870, which attempted to shore up the spiritual authority of the papacy in the face of its loss of the Papal States to a newly unified Italy. In one of the preparatory documents the separation of the institutional Church from other societies was made explicit:

> We teach and declare: The Church has all the marks of a true Society. Christ did not leave this society undefined and without a set form. Rather, he himself gave its existence, and his will determined the form of its existence and gave it its constitution. The Church is not part nor member of any other society and is not mingled in any way with any other society. It is so perfect in itself that it is distinct from all human societies and stands far above them. (Dulles 1988, pp. 36–7)

Avery Dulles points out that some of these themes were taken into the decrees on the papacy adopted by the council, and also used later by subsequent popes such as Leo XIII, Pius XI and Pius XII in their encyclicals. In this outlook spiritual grace is seen as almost a kind of substance inherent in the Church. The pope and bishops, assisted by priests and deacons, are described by some writers in this tradition as if they were engineers opening and shutting the valves of grace. Furthermore, government of the body is placed in the hands of the hierarchy. They govern the flock with pastoral authority, and as Christ's vice-regents impose new laws and precepts under the pain of sin. The Church is not conceived as a democratic or representative society, but as one in which the fullness of power is concentrated in the hands of a ruling class that perpetuates itself by co-option. A preparatory document for Vatican I describes this in the following terms:

> But the Church of Christ is not a community of equals in which all the faithful have the same rights. It is a society of unequals, not only because among the faithful some are clerics and some are laymen, but particularly because there is in the Church the power from God whereby to some it is given to sanctify, teach, and govern, and to others not. (Dulles 1988, p. 38)

This hierarchical Church exists for the benefit of those who belong to it. It is

> a shelter where the faithful are protected against the assaults of the enemy of their souls. The Church is compared to a loving mother who nourishes her infants at the breast, or, more impersonally, to the boat of Peter, which carries the faithful to the farther shore of heaven, provided they remain on board. They have only to be docile and obedient, and to rely on the ministrations of the Church. According to the Vatican I document, 'It is an article of faith that outside the Church no one can be saved . . . Who is not in this ark will perish in the flood.' (Dulles 1988, p. 41)

Mission, then, is the work of bringing the rest of humankind into this divine society. Dulles (pp. 41–2) points out that this outlook is not indifferent to the eternal destiny of the rest of humankind but gives strong support to the missionary effort by which the Church goes out to non-members. But it seeks to save their souls precisely by bringing them into the ark of the institution. Missionary success can be precisely measured, by the number of baptisms performed, by the number of regular worshippers and by the number of those who regularly receive the sacraments.

Vincent Donovan has shown how this outlook guided Roman Catholic missionary work in rural Africa in the latter part of the twentieth century:

> The mission compound with its many necessary buildings . . . stood for the church, the ark and haven of salvation, the repository of grace, and indeed, of God. Outside the compound lay the vast area of tribal life and pagan culture empty of all worth and goodness and holiness and salvation. The missionary process was a movement away from tribal and human life and culture to the church where salvation resided. It was a process of salvation from this world and from human life . . . (Donovan 1982, p. vi)

The Jesus Movement

Moving forward into the twentieth century, other examples of this mission type can be cited from the fringe of the evangelical tradition, in particular the Jesus Movement. John Stott in 1975 described it in the following terms:

> The so-called 'Jesus movement' has encouraged the formation of Christian communes into which zealous young evangelicals withdraw from the wicked world . . . the only contact which such Christians have with the world (which they regard as totally and irredeemably wicked) is to make occasional evangelistic raids into it. Apocalyptic imagery comes naturally to them. The world is like a building on fire, they say; a Christian's only duty is to mount a rescue operation before it is too late. Jesus Christ is coming at any moment; there is no point in tampering with the structures of society, for society is doomed and about to be destroyed. Besides, any attempt to improve society is bound to be unproductive since unrenewed men cannot build a new world. Man's only hope lies in being born again. Only then might society conceivably be reborn. But it is too late now even for that. (Stott 1986, p. 16)

Other examples come from the Seventh Day Adventists, the Jehovah's Witnesses and some independent Pentecostal traditions. Each of these groups goes into the wider society not to try to change it but to recruit individual people out of that society and into their church, so that they may be saved within this ark of safety while everyone else perishes in an imminent deluge.

Stanley Hauerwas

Hauerwas, an influential American Methodist theologian, has produced a more measured and persuasive account of the Church as a separated and distinct community within society. His writings are not dominated by a sense of the eschatological end-times being upon us, but they do draw a sharp distinction between the Church and the surrounding culture. In a popular book, written with William Willimon, *Resident Aliens: Life in the Christian Colony*, he presents one of his strongest expressions of a boundary between the two. Drawing on the work of the Mennonite theologian John Howard Yoder, he draws a distinction between three kinds of church: 'the activist church', which basically accepts the culture in which it lives but seeks to change aspects of it; 'the conversionist church', which calls for an inner conversion while not seeking to change the culture in any significant way; and 'the confessing church', which, following Yoder, he advocates. He describes this confessing church as 'a new people, an alternative *polis*, a countercultural social structure called church. It seeks to influence the world by being the church, that is, by being something the world is not and can never be, lacking the gift of faith and vision . . . The confessing church moves from the activist's church *acceptance* of the culture with a few qualifications, to *rejection* of the culture with a few exceptions' (Hauerwas and Willimon 1989, pp. 46–7, italics mine). The space between church and culture is vividly described in the following:

> The church exists today as resident aliens, an adventurous colony in a society of unbelief. As a society of unbelief, Western culture is devoid of a sense of journey, of adventure, because it lacks belief in much more than the cultivation of an ever-shrinking horizon of self-preservation and self-expression. (ibid., p. 49)

In a later chapter Hauerwas and Willimon describe the role of the minister in this polarized context: 'if we live as a colony of resident aliens within a hostile environment, which, in the most subtle but deadly of ways, corrupts and co-opts us as Christians, the pastor is called to help us gather the resources we need to be the colony of God's righteousness' (ibid., p. 140).

Since the publication of *Resident Aliens* Hauerwas has produced an extensive *corpus* of books and articles that creatively develop his thinking in a range of directions. His theology and ethics have undoubtedly become more nuanced, with less of a sense of wanting to abandon Western society to its own devices and more of a sense of the calling of the Church to be the servant of the world through living its own distinct life. *The Peaceable Kingdom: A Primer in Christian Ethics* is typical, where on the one hand he reaffirms the distinctiveness of the Church's calling: 'The first social ethical task of the church is to be the church – the servant community. Such a claim may sound self-serving until we remember that what makes the church the church is its faithful manifestation of the peaceable kingdom in the world. As such the church does not have a social ethic; the church is a social ethic' (Hauerwas 1983, p. 99). But now he states that the Church 'can never abandon the world to the hopelessness deriving from its rejection of God, but must be a people with a hope sufficiently fervid to sustain the world as well as itself' (ibid., p. 101).

Nevertheless, there is still a sharp distinction between the two and Hauerwas refuses to offer ethical guidance to those who do not enter the congregational life of the Church. Mission, by implication, is still about drawing people into the ark of church membership where they will be able to experience 'the peaceable kingdom'.

Summary of the apostolic Jewish-Christian paradigm

Context
Roman occupation of Palestine;
Jewish apocalyptic expectation of the imminent coming of the messiah.

Authorities
1. Christ's life and teaching
2. Jewish apocalyptic world-view from Hebrew Scriptures
3. Signs and wonders showing the inauguration of the kingdom

Methodology for theology
Exegesis of the Scriptures (e.g. Peter's and Paul's speeches in Acts).

Eschatology
The kingdom is about to come with power. Those who turn away from sin and join the messianic community will be saved.

Christology
Redemptive: Jesus seen as the messiah who is about to return with power and usher in the kingdom of God.

Discipleship
To turn and face the second coming of Christ, leaving behind everything that is contrary to this, joining the community of the saved and calling on others to do the same.

Mission of the Church

An invitation to Jews and then Gentiles to join the messianic community, through repentance and faith in Christ, leading to incorporation in his body, the Church. It is a 'search and rescue' operation whose aim is to give as many people as possible the opportunity to come into the ark of the Church and avoid being drowned in the deluge.

Ministry

'To help the Christian community gather the resources it needs to be the colony of God's righteousness'.

More recent examples

The Anabaptists; Pope Pius IX and documents of Vatican I; the Jesus Movement …
(Stanley Hauerwas).

Debate

How far does this mission type, of mission as filling the ark of salvation, remain consistent with the *missio Christi* and especially with the Galilean principles?

Galilean principles of the *missio Christi* (from p. 33)

1. Contemplative listening, which frames all ministry: listening to God, to other people, to oneself, especially in times of prayer and retreat.

2. Addressing society as a whole, at points where people live and work, including and especially the marginalized. This results in being received and accepted by some but rejected and opposed by others.

3. Pointing to the inaugurated yet still awaited kingdom, in word and in surprising saving deed (symbolic actions) which address the actual needs of people (both individual and structural); but without publicizing the wonders.   .

4. Calling for a personal response by all to the coming of this kingdom.

5. Doing all this through a collaborative team, who themselves are powerless and vulnerable and must suffer the consequences.

One response

It is clear from the above that some of these principles were expressed within the mission of the apostles. The fourth principle is one, because both Peter and Paul in their initial and defining speeches as apostles end their words by calling on their audience to turn and commit themselves to the new reality they are proclaiming: 'Repent, and be baptized every one of you in the name of Jesus Christ for the forgiveness of your sins; and you shall receive the gift of the Holy Spirit' (Acts 2.38; see also 10.43–8; for Paul see 13.38–9). When it is recalled that in the opening of his speech the pouring out of the Spirit was linked with the arrival of the last days, it is apparent that he was following Jesus' example and calling for a personal response from the members of his audience to the coming of God's kingdom.

There is also evidence of the collaborative nature of the apostolic mission. One example is the way the eleven stood with Peter when he made his speech on the day of Pentecost (2.14); another is the way the crowd responded to him and them collectively (2.37); and a third is how those who were converted devoted themselves to the teaching and fellowship 'of the apostles', showing the existence of a unified community (2.42; see also vv. 43–7 and 4.32–7). Subsequent decisions about church matters were made as a body, such as the decision to appoint seven 'deacons' to assist with the daily distribution (6.2–3), and over the deep division on whether to allow Gentiles to be admitted into the fellowship without requiring them to be circumcised and become Jews. This issue was resolved by a council of the apostles and elders (15.6) in which, surprisingly, it was not Peter but another apostle, James, who provided a solution to the crisis (15.13ff.). The decision to send Paul and Barnabas to Antioch with a letter was again a collective one (15.22). In all these ways and others it is clear the fourth Galilean principle found strong expression in the life of the apostolic Church.

Furthermore the fifth Galilean principle is in evidence at many points in the narrative of Acts. The apostles and other disciples are described as being in prayer and worship at many points, first in the upper room (1.14, 24–5; 2.1–4; 4.24–31), sometimes in the Temple (2.46; 3.1) and sometimes in each other's homes (2.42, 46). These examples also show the apostles turning to prayer when decisions need to be made, and this pattern is repeated at many points throughout the whole book. A sense of the apostolic Church seeking and listening to the promptings of the Spirit comes through in a number of places (e.g. 4.29–31;

8.14–17; 13.1–3). So it seems clear that the mission of the apostles was framed by genuine worship and prayer, with an openness to the promptings of the Spirit.

What of the central and key third principle, of pointing to the inaugurated yet still awaited kingdom, in ways that address the actual needs of people? The case study of Paul, drawing on the recent scholarship of N. T. Wright, showed how Paul understood the Church to be inhabiting both the current age, which was coming to an end, and the new age of the inaugurated kingdom of God. An important continuity with Jesus' teaching, which spoke of the kingdom being both inaugurated and awaited, therefore exists at this point. But did apostolic mission address the actual needs of people? At one level it clearly did because the book of Acts describes a number of wonderful and unexpected healings that took place through the ministry of the apostles. But, at another level, we have already seen how there was no attempt by the apostolic Church to fight against the evil of slavery in the Roman empire or other forms of structural oppression. The reason for this was understandable, that with the expectation that the current age was about to end there was no reason for the Church to engage in such longer-term political campaigns. The whole Roman empire was about to be destroyed anyway! But in comparison with Jesus' mission, where according to N. T. Wright there *was* a political agenda of reforming the corporate relationships of the Jewish community, as seen in his conflict with the Pharisees, we see a significant contrast. Apostolic mission, for its own understandable reasons, did not (and, in the more recent examples mentioned above, does not) seek to address the corporate needs of the whole community through political struggle. On this important point the third Galilean principle is not fulfilled by this type of mission.

This is also, arguably, a failure to fulfil the second principle with its requirement that the missioner addresses the whole of society and especially the marginalized. While Jesus sought out everyone in Jewish society, including the marginalized, symbolized by his calling twelve disciples to represent the twelve tribes of Israel, the apostles who travelled outside Palestine did not do the same within the wider society of the Roman empire. Acts reports that Peter and Paul invariably went first to the Jewish communities in the cities they visited, and preached to them and to those Gentiles who were on the edges of these communities. It was only slowly and gradually that the focus of apostolic mission shifted from Jews to Gentiles as relations with synagogues deteriorated. The apostles probably had no choice as there was no forum in which they could have addressed every group within the empire: Graeco-Roman society was simply too vast and variegated. Nevertheless, compared to the scope of Jesus' mission within his own society, the apostolic mission possibly shows a narrowing of the range of people who were approached.

Furthermore, it can be argued that in general seeing the Church as an ark or as a colony of resident aliens (in Hauerwas' language) *restricts* its appeal to those who are not within its current fellowship. Sharp boundaries between those within and those without creates a sense of exclusion for those on the outside and makes it less likely that they will be drawn into the fellowship: they come to see the Church as being for 'them' rather than for 'us'. This reinforces the sense that this type of mission is not broad enough in the range of people it seeks to reach.

Out of the five Galilean principles, therefore, the apostolic mission type clearly fulfils three of them. But there are questions over the extent to which it fulfils the third principle, especially over the way it does not address structural causes of suffering, and also over the way that through drawing sharp boundaries between church and world it makes fulfilment of the second principle very difficult.

As the first century ended and the second century began, the Church moved further and further away from the Jewish world of Palestine and into the wider Graeco-Roman world around the Mediterranean. As the next chapter will show, this Hellenistic world had a very different understanding of reality and especially of eschatology. A different Christian paradigm would be needed and, within that, a different type of Christian mission to reach the people of that far-flung world.

Discussion questions

Are there communities today which are on the brink of collapsing, or where some external danger is about to overwhelm them, where this type of mission may be very appropriate?
What might the strengths and weaknesses of this type of mission be within your own local context?

Further reading

Bosch, David J. (1991), *Transforming Mission: Paradigm Shifts in Theology of Mission*, Orbis

Bradstock, Andrew, and Christopher Rowland, eds. (2002), *Radical Christian Writings: A Reader*, Blackwell

Caird, G. B. (1955), *The Apostolic Age*, Duckworth

Donovan, Vincent (1982), *Christianity Rediscovered: An Epistle from the Masai*, SCM Press

Dulles, Avery, SJ (1988), *Models of the Church*, 2nd edn, Gill & Macmillan

Dunn, James D. G. (1997), *The Theology of Paul the Apostle*, Eerdmans

Frend, W. H. C. (1984) *The Rise of Christianity*, DLT

Hauerwas, Stanley (1983), *The Peaceable Kingdom: A Primer in Christian Ethics*, University of Notre Dame Press

Hauerwas, Stanley, and William Willimon (1989), *Resident Aliens: Life in the Christian Colony*, Abingdon Press

Küng, Hans (1995), *Christianity: Its Essence and History*, SCM Press

Little, Franklin H. (2000), *The Anabaptist View of the Church (Dissent and Nonconformity)*, Baptist Standard Bearer

Murray, Stuart (2004a), *Post Christendom*, Paternoster

Murray, Stuart (2004b), *Church after Christendom*, Paternoster

Senior, D., and C. Stuhlmueller (1983), *The Biblical Foundation of Mission*, Orbis

Stott, John (1986), *Christian Mission in the Modern World*, Kingsway

Tomkins, Stephen (2004), *Paul and His World*, Lion

Wright, N. T. (2005), *Paul: Fresh Perspectives*, SPCK

6

Radiating Eternal Truth Hellenistic Orthodox Mission

There is a story in the *Russian Primary Chronicle* of how Vladimir, Prince of Kiev, while still a pagan, desired to know which was the true religion, and therefore sent his followers to visit the various countries of the world in turn. They went first to the Moslem Bulgars of the Volga, but observing that these when they prayed gazed around them like men possessed, the Russians continued on their way dissatisfied. 'There is no joy among them,' they reported to Vladimir . . . Travelling next to Germany and Rome, they found the worship more satisfactory, but complained that here too it was without beauty. Finally they journeyed to Constantinople, and here at last, as they attended the Divine Liturgy in the great Church of the Holy Wisdom, they discovered what they desired. 'We knew not whether we were in heaven or on earth, for surely there is no such splendour or beauty anywhere upon earth. We cannot describe it to you: only this we know, that God dwells there among men, and that their service surpasses the worship of all other places. For we cannot forget that beauty. (Ware 1963, p. 269)

These words, describing events leading to the conversion of Russia at the turn of the first millennium, take us into a very different world from the Jewish Christianity of the apostles and they introduce a whole new paradigm of Christian life and thought. This was a paradigm born in the Hellenistic Christianity of the second to fourth centuries which continued in the Middle East and Eastern Europe until the conversion of Russia. It has remained the dominant paradigm within the Orthodox tradition ever since. It is centred on the liturgy of the Church:

> The Holy Liturgy is something that embraces two worlds at once, for both in heaven and on earth the Liturgy is one and the same – one altar, one sacrifice, one presence. In every place of worship, however humble its outward appearance, as the faithful gather to perform the Eucharist, they are taken up into the 'heavenly places'; in every place of worship when the Holy Sacrifice is offered, not merely the local congregation are present, but the Church universal – the saints, the angels, the Mother of God, and Christ himself. 'Now the celestial powers are present with us, and worship invisibly.' (Ware 1963, p. 270, quoting the Orthodox Liturgy of the Pre-sanctified)

After introducing the origins of this rich and influential paradigm, this chapter will explore its distinctive approach to mission, an approach radically and creatively different from those which preceded and followed it.

Background: the rise of Platonic philosophy within Christianity

Contrary to expectation, the Lord did not return within the lifetime of the first disciples and apostles. There is evidence from the New Testament that this precipitated a minor crisis for the Church. The epistle 2 Peter describes how some were coming to 'scoff' at the Church because of the non-appearance of the Lord (2 Peter 3.3). The author shows concern at the delay but reassures his readers that the Lord's timing is not the same as earthly timing and that the purpose of the delay is to give more people the opportunity to repent (vv. 8–9). He believes the end of the age is still to come but has no idea when it may be (v. 10).

But the end of the age did not take place and the Church was forced to rethink its eschatology. Meanwhile it was spreading and expanding into a predominantly Greek-speaking and -thinking culture in Asia Minor and Greece. Christians started living, thinking and communicating within a milieu that was very different from the one they had come from. In Palestinian Jewish culture, with its roots in the Hebrew Scriptures, there was an emphasis on activity / practice / righteous living as the key to salvation (as, for example, in Amos 5.24, where the prophet calls for justice and righteousness to roll down like waters). In the Hellenistic world there were some very different outlooks in place, one of which was Neoplatonism, an outlook which had a big impact on Christianity. To understand this point of view we can go back to Plato himself (427–347 BC), the disciple and recorder of Socrates, who was the pre-eminent influence on this way of philosophical thinking. A passage from his dialogue *Timaeus* is revealing:

> If the heart of man has been set on the love of learning and true wisdom and he has exercised that part of himself above all, he is surely bound to have thoughts immortal and divine, if he shall lay hold upon truth, nor can he fail to possess immortality in the fullest meaning that human nature admits; and because he is always devoutly cherishing the divine part and maintaining the guardian genius that dwells with him in good estate, he must needs be happy above all. (Charlesworth 2002, p. 19)

In this passage it is significant that union with the divine and immortality is seen as being achieved not at some future day of judgement, but in the here and now, through learning and the acquisition of wisdom. In Plato's philosophy generally the divine is portrayed as an immortal or ever-present reality, called the realm of 'the forms' and equated with beauty, truth, goodness, virtue, love and other supreme qualities. It is regarded as the real world, eternal and unchanging, while the visible and material world is one that changes and decays, a world of dust and ashes and of mere appearances that are passing away. In opposition to Greek mythology, which portrayed heroism, glory in battle, and strength as the supreme virtues, Socrates and Platonism generally presented learning, knowledge, wisdom and belief as the key to immortality and happiness.

The allegory of the cave, from Plato's *Republic* (7.7), is a famous portrayal of this point of view, where the material and visible world is equated with moving shadows on the walls of the cave which shackled prisoners spend their day watching. We are those prisoners. The *real* world, of the eternal forms, is equated with what is outside the cave and bathed in bright sunshine. It is through philosophy that a prisoner is freed of their shackles and enabled to move out of the shadows and into the sunshine of the real and eternal world.

This philosophical world-view, with its belief in timeless knowledge as the key to salvation, became generally disseminated around the ancient world of the first century as Neoplatonism and began to influence the early Christian community when it began to move out of the confines of Palestinian Judaism and into cosmopolitan cities such as Caesarea, Antioch in Syria and Ephesus. It was highly influential in the major centres of learning in the ancient world at this time, such as Alexandria in Egypt as well Athens and Ephesus. Judaism had already been engaging with Platonism when the Church began to spread through the Hellenistic world, not least through the Jewish philosopher Philo (*c.*20 AD – 50 AD) in Alexandria. It is possible to see the influence of Platonic language and ways of thinking in the book of Wisdom in the Apocrypha:

> The beginning of wisdom is the most sincere desire for instruction, and concern for instruction is love of her, and love of her is the keeping of her laws, and giving heed to her laws is assurance of immortality, and immortality brings one near to God; so the desire for wisdom leads to a kingdom. (6.17–20)

With its emphasis on the eternal being an ever-present reality behind the appearances of this world, Neoplatonism can also be detected in some of the later New Testament writings. It is seen in the way they shift their presentation of Christian teaching away from the expectation of a future judgement and salvation at the parousia (which was prominent in 1 Thessalonians and Matthew 25, for example), to an assertion that this judgement and salvation were already a present reality. This is the shift from a future eschatology to a realized eschatology. John's Gospel presents one of the best examples with its emphasis on what Christ has already accomplished and what he offers here and now:

> Those who believe in him are not condemned; but those who do not believe are condemned *already*, because they have not believed in the name of the only Son of God. And this is the judgement, that the light *has* come into the world, and people loved darkness rather than light because their deeds were evil. (3.18–19, italics mine)

Very truly, I tell you, anyone who hears my word and believes him who sent me *has* eternal life, and does not come under judgement, but *has* passed from death to life. Very truly, I tell you, the hour is coming, *and now is here*, when the dead will hear the voice of the Son of God, and those who hear will live. (5.24–5, italics mine)

Furthermore, in one of the key verses of the Gospel and one of the most famous verses in the New Testament, it is the interior virtue of belief rather than the practice of righteousness and justice (which, as seen, are supreme virtues within the Hebrew Scriptures) which is presented as the heart of Christian living and the gateway to eternal life: 'For God so loved the world that he gave his only Son, so that everyone who believes in him may not perish but may have eternal life' (3.16).

All of this shows the start of a paradigm shift in Christian thinking, the first such shift in the history of the Christian movement, from one mainly influenced by Hebrew ways of thinking to one mainly influenced by these Hellenistic ways of thinking.

The Apologists, who were Greek-speaking theologians, show the next stage in this development. One of the first and most influential was Justin Martyr (c.100–c.165), who taught in Ephesus and Rome, where he opened a Christian school. In the face of persecution by the Roman authorities he sought to show that Christianity was a true philosophy, better able than any other to express the nature of truth. He developed the doctrine of the 'generative' or 'germinative' Word (*logos*), who had sown the seed of truth in all people and who had become incarnate in Christ in order to teach all people the whole truth. Justin Martyr was positing a fundamental continuity between philosophy and Christ, using the terminology of the one to describe the other. He also employed a number of ideas from the Neoplatonism of Philo to interpret and explain the Hebrew Scriptures.

Among the church fathers Clement of Alexandria (c.150–c.215) and Origen (c.185–254) interweaved Neoplatonism with Christian thought. Origen, who was educated in Neoplatonic philosophy in Alexandria, wrote the following revealing letter to his former student Gregory Thaumaturgus, at around 230 AD:

I wish to ask you to extract from the philosophy of the Greeks what may serve as a course of study or a preparation for Christianity, and from geometry and astronomy what will serve to explain the sacred scriptures, in order that all that the sons of the philosophers are wont to say about geometry and music, grammar, rhetoric, and astronomy, as fellow-helpers to philosophy, we may say about philosophy itself, in relation to Christianity. (Bevans and Schroeder 2004, p. 96)

In his works, many of which are now lost, Origen presented a fundamental and creative reinterpretation of the Christian faith in terms of Greek philosophy, and he is sometimes called the first systematic theologian. The stories of the Bible were also read allegorically, carrying a meaning which needed to be unlocked from the text of Scripture through the application of a key. This was a deeper, philosophical meaning. (For a readable, informative and enthusiastic introduction to Origen's theology see Hill 2003, pp. 37–57.)

In all of this we see the explaining of the Christian faith to a Greek culture, with an emphasis on the way Christianity expresses ancient truth. Greek philosophy is positively evaluated as a 'schoolmaster' that can lead the Greeks to Christ.

More important still, St Augustine of Hippo, who would become a hugely influential figure on the development of theology in the Western Church of the Middle Ages, was radically influenced by Neoplatonic ways of thinking. He interpreted his conversion as the result of his quest for wisdom, and in his writings often speaks of having arrived in the 'haven of philosophy'. 'Christianity' and 'true philosophy' are practically synonymous terms in his early writings (R. A. Markus, quoted in Charlesworth 2002, p. 28; for more on the Christian Platonists and Augustine see ibid., pp. 50–5).

What impact did this change of outlook have on the Church? There is clearly a fundamental shift taking place: whereas in the apostolic period, under the influence of Jewish beliefs, the Church saw itself as a community that was living between past and future events, and specifically between the history of Israel, which had reached its fulfilment in the life, death and resurrection of Christ, and the end of the age and the second coming of Christ, now it was defining itself in a very different way: Christianity was all about holding right beliefs, which can be definitively stated as doctrines that articulate eternal truths. These beliefs had become the key to salvation.

This is one reason why the development of creeds became centrally important to the Church. It was crucial that everyone knew the right doctrine so that they would have access to eternal life. The story of the development of the creeds is complex and protracted but there are three crucial moments:

- The Council of Nicaea, 325, which defined the being of God as 'three *hypostases* in one *ousia*' (often translated as three persons in one substance – the doctrine of the Trinity)

- The first Council of Constantinople, 381, which adopted the Nicene Creed
- The Council of Chalcedon, 451, which attempted to define with finality and clarity the nature of Christ as fully human and fully divine.

These developments show the Christian faith being defined and accepted as a set of beliefs, to be learnt and assimilated within the mind of the believer. Salvation is all about the progress of the soul as it learns and assimilates these doctrines and becomes united with the immortal wisdom of God. This is at the core of the Hellenistic paradigm and remains important within Orthodox thinking to this day (see, for example, Ware 1963, pp. 216ff.).

Christian mission within the Hellenistic paradigm

How is the true philosophy of Christianity to be passed on? For Hellenistic Christianity, which became the forebear of the Orthodox tradition, the answer has always been through the life of the Church. It is the Church that draws people into its worship, teaches them the doctrine of the faith and allows them to experience the reality of eternal life through its sacraments. The Church, in other words, is the expression of mission: 'In Orthodox thinking, mission is thoroughly *Church-centred*.' Bosch continues that this 'has its roots in early Eastern theology, where an ever stronger accent was put on ecclesiology. The conviction gradually grew that the church was the kingdom of God on earth and that to be in the church was the same as being in the kingdom . . . the church is the dispenser of salvific light and the mediator of power for renewal which produces life' (Bosch 1991, p. 207). Quoting the great Orthodox theologian Alexander Schmemann, Bosch writes, 'the basic elements of an answer to the question about Orthodox understanding of mission must be looked for in its "doctrine and experience of the Church." Mission is "part of the nature of the church" (ibid., p. 207).

This has important implications for the practice of mission: 'Under no circumstances may any individual, or group of individuals, embark upon a missionary venture without being sent and supported by the church.' Bosch quotes N. A Nissiotis: '"Christ must be preached within His Historical reality, His Body in the Spirit, without which there is neither Christ nor the Gospel. Outside the context of the Church, evangelism remains a humanism or a temporary psychological enthusiasm"' (ibid., p. 207).

The liturgy becomes central for mission within this understanding. It is through the liturgy that the Church gathers and schools people so that they learn and assimilate eternal knowledge. This is seen pre-eminently in the way the catechumenate developed. This pre-baptismal course of preparation for new Christians began in the Hellenistic Church, probably in the fourth century. There was so much emphasis on the new Christians being taught the right knowledge that the course was spread over 40 days, in the period leading up to Easter, when they would be baptized. (This 40-day preparation was the origin of the season of Lent.)

Mission, then, was all about bringing people into the ordered liturgical community of the Church where they could be schooled in the doctrine and truth of heaven and given the opportunity to ascend into divine truth.

But this was not a purely intellectual exercise. The *experience* of the liturgy had a crucial part to play:

As church of the Easter light and liturgy it sees its main task in enlightening the pagans who are to receive God's light through the liturgy. The major manifestation of the missionary activity of the Orthodox church lies in its celebration of the liturgy. The light of mercy that shines in the liturgy should act as center of attraction to those who still live in the darkness of paganism. (K. Rose, in Bosch 1991, p. 207)

In helpful elucidation Bosch continues,

In the Orthodox perspective mission is thus centripetal rather than centrifugal, organic rather than organized. It 'proclaims' the gospel through doxology and liturgy. The witnessing community is the community in worship; in fact, the worshipping community is in and of itself an act of witness . . . People are not called simply to know Christ, to gather around him, or to submit to his will; 'they are called to participate in his glory'. (ibid., pp. 208–9)

This is the doctrine of *theosis*, which states that through the incarnation humanity can have union with God, 'a continuing state of adoration, prayer, thanksgiving, worship, and intercession, as well as meditation and contemplation of the triune God and God's infinite love' (ibid., p. 209). It is this which leads Orthodox believers to say that the liturgy of the Church becomes 'heaven on earth'. In the liturgy, then, *eternal truth radiates into the world*, and this is the heart of Orthodox mission.

All of this means that mission was not restricted to one or two aspects of the Church's life but was understood to be expressed by the whole life of the Church: as Bevans and Schroeder have written, 'every ministry was missionary, because at this point the entire church saw itself in this way. Mission was not a part of the church's reality, but was its very essence' (Bevans and Schroeder 2004, p. 83).

But how did those who did not go to church hear the gospel? Casual and informal witness became central to spreading the word, a 'gossiping the gospel'. Celsus, a second-century critic of Christianity, gives us a graphic picture of informal evangelization being carried out by woodcarvers, cobblers, laundry workers and uneducated people both in private homes and during other daily encounters (ibid., pp. 86–92). All of this was supported and extended by what Bevans and Schroeder call 'secondary models of mission', by which they mean the evangelists, bishops, apologists and teachers who travelled across the ancient world, connecting one church with another. There were also the martyrs, who through the shedding of their blood bore witness to the truth of Hellenistic Christianity (ibid., pp. 83–6).

An important difference from the ark type, over the drawing of boundaries, is apparent at this point. Whereas in that approach to mission the key boundary was between those people who were within the saved community of the Church and those who were without, for this type of mission the key boundary was not one between people but between earth and heaven, a boundary symbolized by the iconostasis, the wooden screen dividing the nave from the sanctuary. This screen has a central gateway that is only opened during the liturgy, and the opening of the gateway during the liturgy with the bringing of the sacramental elements out into the congregation shows the people crossing this boundary and experiencing the glory of heaven. Everyone within the community is invited to do so: the Church is not an ark for the saved but an open door for the whole community. Mission is directed toward and inclusive of all people and, indeed, of all creation, as Schmemann implies:

> State, society, culture, nature itself, are real *objects* of mission and not a neutral 'milieu' in which the only task of the Church is to reserve its own inner freedom, to maintain its 'religious life' . . . In the world of incarnation

nothing 'neutral' remains, nothing can be taken away from the Son of Man. (Bosch 1991, p. 210)

This acceptance of society as a whole, without the sharp drawing of boundaries, has also meant that the Orthodox tradition has not generally tried to change society by adopting programmes of reform. It has often been a conservative tradition, advocating contemplation rather than action as the way forward. It has often become closely associated with the governing authorities, within both the Greek and Russian traditions, resulting in church and society penetrating and permeating each other. To Western eyes it has sometimes seemed to be indifferent to the realities of suffering and injustice in the world. However, Orthodox theologians emphasize that the liturgy of the Church continues in the 'second liturgy', which takes place after the service in the world (see Bosch 1991, p. 210). The love that is revealed in the liturgy is to be revealed as well in the daily lives of those who have participated in it (Figure 4).

There were at least two major developments within the Hellenistic paradigm. The first was the Gnostic movement, which grew from about the year 120. This

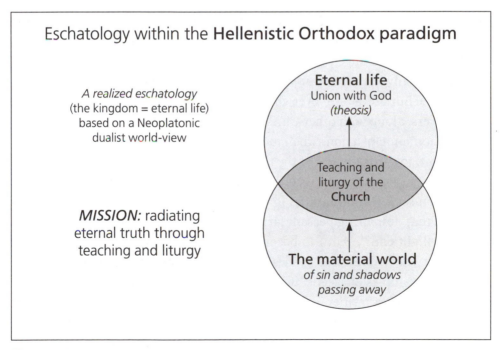

Figure 4

was very influential in the early Church but was condemned by the theologian and bishop Irenaeus (*c*.130–*c*.200) and was repressed by church authorities with increasing zeal. It was an extreme form of Neoplatonism, in which the visible world of matter and flesh was regarded as evil and the invisible world of divine knowledge was regarded as good. Salvation was all about escaping from the prison of matter and flesh and ascending into this realm of esoteric knowledge. The believer had to join a Gnostic (i.e. knowing) community before they could be inducted into this secret knowledge. For Christian Gnostics Jesus was the saviour, but his humanity was understood to be only a kind of veneer covering his real nature, which was divine (which teaching is often described as a docetic Christology). (For an introduction to Christian Gnosticism see Pagels 2006.)

The second development was the emergence of monasticism, which has had a huge impact in the Western Church as well as in the East.

Case study: St Antony of Egypt and the founding of monasticism

St Antony of Egypt (*c*.251–356) may not seem an appropriate example of mission because he seemed to withdraw from the world rather than go into it, but ironically he contributed hugely to the spread of Christianity in the Graeco-Roman world, especially in the rural areas. When the emperor Diocletian seized power in 284 the Church was still overwhelmingly an urban institution. Antony and his followers, along with other Christians in North Africa, helped to create the new phenomenon of a non-urban monastic Christianity.

In Egypt, towards the end of the third century (270–300), heavy taxation by the Roman authorities led to economic stress, which forced many poor people to abandon settled communities for a precarious livelihood in the desert. It is recorded that despairing peasant farmers asked an oracle 'Shall I flee?', 'When shall my flight end?', 'Am I to become a beggar?' (Frend 1984, p. 422). Some Christians who had fled into the desert during earlier persecutions stayed there, providing examples of ascetic life which others might follow. In *c*.270 Antony, a young Christian farmer, inherited a considerable holding from his parents in Coma, Upper Egypt. One Sunday he was at a service in his village church. The lesson was from Matthew 19 and contained the Lord's command to the rich young man, 'Go, sell what you possess and give to the poor, and you will have treasure in heaven; and come, follow me' (Matt. 19.21). There was to be no allegorical interpretation for Antony: he took the words literally and acted at once. He placed his sister in a convent and left his home to establish himself as a solitary on the edge of the village where the desert would come to the very edge of the cultivated land. There he remained for fifteen years. Then he left the sparse company of the local hermits and went to the Arabian mountains on the east side of the Nile. There, at Pispir, he remained in an abandoned fort until the outbreak of the Great Persecution in 303. Here he underwent a series of temptations usually associated with the hermit life. He lived by gardening and mat-making and combined severe austerity with an awareness of the love of God.

At the end of this period he left his solitude to guide disciples who had gathered around him. They believed they had come into the desert to fight demons, who were thought to have infested the deserts. They were joined by many small landholders who had thrown up their farms as a hopeless proposition in the face of heavy taxation from the Roman authorities and violence and extortion from the soldiers. From his monastery he went to Alexandria in 311 to encourage confessors during the persecution of Maximin. But Antony's community never advocated violent opposition to the authorities. He had written contact with the first Christian emperors, Constantine (who legalized Christianity in 313 in the Edict of Milan) and Constantius, and he spent much time forwarding petitions to officials, sure that he would receive a favourable response. His surviving letters include one to the Emperor Constantine. A bond of respect and loyalty was established. So Antony and his community followed the tradition of the Egyptian and Syrian bishops by giving loyalty to the emperor. And Orthodoxy, as it had been formulated by Athanasius against the Arians, was upheld: 'Loyalty, above all to Athanasius and his memory, silent dignity, and complete assurance of their position and way of life made the Coptic monks a formidable influence in the eastern Roman Empire' (Frend 1984, p. 576).

In 355 Antony went again to Alexandria, this time to refute the Arians. The philosophers were impressed; he was reputed to be a miracle worker and many were converted by him. Many of his sayings are preserved and there is a monastic Rule in his name which contains at least some elements of his teaching. He is sometimes described as the founder of monasticism. (He was very popular in the Middle Ages and a Legend was composed in English verse, which is depicted on the backs of the stalls of Carlisle Cathedral.)

Antony had many imitators. His brand of monasticism spread to the Nile

Delta and south-west of Alexandria, and in Upper Egypt to the east of the Nile. Under Pachomius there were nine monasteries housing several hundred monks. By the year 390 nearly fifty thousand monks would congregate to celebrate Easter.

Frend provides the following commentary on all of this:

Antony's motives were partly religious, to live entirely by literal obedience to Scripture, but there was also a social motive. Athanasius, who wrote a life of Antony, says that he despairingly asked 'Why do the rich grind the faces of the poor?' Hard work for his own subsistence needs was his practice. He himself had been a failure in early life and had little use for the ways of secular society. His settlement of ascetics in the mountains became a refuge for those fleeing from the extortions of tax collectors, whose 'grumbles' he records. This social motive was combined with an ascetic tradition that reached back to the dawn of Christianity, to John the Baptist, and to Jesus' example of seeking out a solitary place for prayer in the mountains or wilderness. Almost for the first time in three centuries the Lord's commands were being accepted literally by Christ's followers. (Frend 1984, p. 423)

Elsewhere Frend writes that the rise of the monastic movement would eventually lead to the total disintegration of rural paganism in the entire Graeco-Roman world. And following Frend, Bosch comments that,

When Christianity became the official religion of the Empire and persecutions ended, the monk succeeded the martyr as the expression of unqualified witness and protest against worldliness. Since the fourth century the history of the church on the move, particularly in the East, was essentially also the history of monasticism. In fact, from the very beginning of monasticism, the most daring and most efficient missionaries were the monks. (Bosch 1991, p. 202)

While at first, then, it may have seemed that Antony was reverting to the ark type in his expression of mission, by withdrawing from the corruption and violence of the world, it is clear from the way his monasticism developed that this was not the case. He developed many contacts with the Roman authorities and became involved in theological controversy and church life in general. All this shows that he was not interested in providing an ark of safety but was upholding the Hellenistic view of the Church as an open door to heaven for the community on earth. The difference was that Antony believed this door should be away from the worldliness of the urban centres and be in places where he and his brothers would be unencumbered to fight the real battle, the spiritual struggle against the demons and temptations that resided in the deserts. It was in the wilderness, as John the Baptist and Jesus had found, that the door to heaven could be kept open for all to pass through. In its simplicity and integrity this was a powerful renewal of the Hellenistic approach to mission.

Note on Celtic monasticism
In many ways the early Celtic and Anglo-Saxon monasticism of the British Isles derives from Antony and Hellenistic monasticism. For a description of this movement which also shows its continuing relevance as an approach to mission today see Bradley 2000. See also Olsen 2003, pp. 44–8.

Some recent expressions of the type

Orthodoxy is today numerically the second largest part of the Christian world, having some 200 million members. It is present in many parts of the Middle East as well as being the largest religious grouping in Romania, Greece, Serbia, Bulgaria, and the Ukraine and Russia (where it has some 50 million members). With emigration to the West, many Orthodox churches are now increasingly strong in Western Europe and North America. This is not the place to describe the complex history and varied manifestations of Orthodoxy, but it is appropriate to see how its influence has spread beyond its own churches in the Western Church. Within Anglicanism, for example, its influence can be detected at a number of points in its history, not least in the years following the Russian revolution when many Orthodox clergy and people fled from Russia and set up congregations in London and other Western cities:

> The Easterners succeeded in communicating, especially to the disciples of the Oxford Movement, the beauty within their heritage; the sense of a living way of worship; the affection for the quiet meditative prayer of the heart; the sense of mystery in the universe and of God as too high for human definition;

and the powerful sense of the communion of the saints, fostered by the icons and by a stylized tradition of art and ornament. (Chadwick 1990, pp. 287–8)

For many within Anglicanism this has resulted in a heightened understanding of the way doctrine and worship go hand in hand, summed up in the Latin phrase *lex orandi lex credendi* (the law of prayer is the law of belief, or 'how a person worships shows what the person believes').

Michael Ramsey's theology

A specific example of this influence is seen in the thought of Michael Ramsey (1904–88), who was Archbishop of Canterbury in the 1960s. Ramsey himself provided the following declaration of gratitude to Orthodoxy in a lecture to an Orthodox audience in the University of Athens in 1962:

> Now that personal contact [between Anglicans and Orthodox] has become frequent we have come to know Orthodox theology not only as a collection of books but as it is alive in living persons and in the Holy Liturgy. That Liturgy conveys to us the glory of the Resurrection. If in the West we have tended to think of the Liturgy as the infinite condescension of the Lord of Heaven in coming to earth to be the food of our souls, in the East we find that the Liturgy lives and moves in heaven, where Christ is, and the Church is lifted into heaven with him. So too the Liturgy of St Chrysostom makes vivid to us the Communion of Saints . . . [it] shows the saints not as individual mediators but as members with us and all the departed in the one family of God, and as it is Christ's own glory which is reflected in the saints to honour them is to honour, supremely, him. We see your Church as the Church of the Resurrection, the Church of the Communion of Saints. (Ramsey 1964, p. 69)

This debt translated into a renewed understanding of the heavenly dimension of Christian worship within Ramsey's own thinking. In one of his most famous addresses, delivered to ordinands on the day before they were made priests, and in terms that recall the quotations from the Orthodox writers at the beginning of this chapter, he described the Eucharist as a place where the company of heaven and earth meet in communion, an earthly place where the eternal reign of Christ can be found: 'The Eucharist is the supreme way in which the people of Christ are, through our great high priest, with God with the world around on their hearts. So great is the Eucharistic mystery that it is easy for the people to miss some aspects of it.' Ramsey then described the missionary role of the priest within this company:

> The priest will help the people to realize both the Godward and manward aspects of the liturgy. He will show them that it is more than their table-fellowship with one another, for it is their sharing in the worship of heaven with Blessed Mary and the Saints. He will show them that they are brought near to the awful reality of the death of the Lord on Calvary as well as to his heavenly glory. He will show them that there is no separated realm of piety, for the Christ upon whom they feed is one with the pains of humanity around them. ('Man of Prayer', in Ramsey 1972, p. 16)

This theology of the communion of saints has influenced not only those who had direct contact with Ramsey but countless others who have been set and read his books as part of their preparation for ordination.

Owen Chadwick adds that when Athenagoras the Ecumenical Patriarch of Constantinople (the most senior bishop in Orthodoxy) came to visit Ramsey at Lambeth Palace in 1967, 'Never since Theodore of Tarsus in the seventh century was there an Archbishop of Canterbury so capable of penetrating and valuing what the Ecumenical Patriarch stood for, and never before was there an Ecumenical Patriarch so capable of penetrating and valuing what the Archbishop of Canterbury stood for' (Chadwick 1990, pp. 291–2; see ch. 12 for biographical details; see Allchin 1995 for further discussion of Ramsey and the Orthodox tradition).

Taizé

A different and widely popular example of the Hellenistic mission type in a Western setting is the Taizé movement. This has not sprung from any kind of evangelistic campaign but has resulted from the centripetal attraction of the Taizé community of brothers, especially through its contemplative worship. Over the years it has drawn an increasing number of young people from across

Europe to its worship and common life in the village of Taizé in France. It has also sponsored gatherings of large numbers of young people in cities across Europe.

The community itself was founded by the Swiss layman Roger Schutz in 1940. He, his sister and others became involved in providing a safe house with care and hospitality for refugees, including Jews, during the war. After the war they looked after orphans and later welcomed German prisoners of war. In 1949 the members of the community made commitments of sharing and simplicity of life, and since then they have steadily grown in numbers. There are now 100 brothers, Protestants and Catholics, from many countries, who go and live in various trouble spots around the world as well as in Taizé itself. Most remarkably, the community welcomes thousands of visitors, mostly young people, to the village every summer, for prayer, Bible study, worship, and workshops on the issues of the day. The community worship is one of the most distinctive and important aspects of these gatherings, with use of meditative chants, candles, icons and an atmosphere of prayer surrounding everything. Many of the visitors say they come for the peace and illumination they find there. The musical style of the chanting has become so popular that it is now used in worship all around the world. For many the atmosphere that it creates is a tangible sign of the peace and eternity of heaven breaking into and reconciling the turmoil of humanity on earth:

> Here are people who pray, and who are alert to news arriving from every continent, be it a drought in Africa, or a coup d'état elsewhere, or a riot in India . . . In the common prayer morning and evening you hear people and situations being brought before God, and suddenly you realise that this is communion; it is an expression of concern and at the same time 'a sharing in the suffering of Christ for his Body'.

The participation in a mystical communion reminiscent of Orthodoxy is central to the Taizé experience:

> The whole celebration of God in prayer here is full of this challenge to 'live the communion Christ offers and so become people of communion for others'. Silence and beauty – a space for contemplation – the Church of Reconciliation [in Taizé] welcomes, with the sunlight streaming in golden patterns

down the walls, or in the silent darkness of evening. Small lights draw our gaze towards the altar, to the icon of Mary, to the tabernacle. The bells peal, songs fill the silence, then release it again – a long pause holding us all in a common prayer: 'Come, Lord Jesus, come now for us all, come for every person, come for all mankind . . .' On Sunday the Eucharist, a sharing in the gifts of Christ's Body and Blood. Late at night you will still find people there, sometimes many people, in prayer, prostrate and simply waiting. (Balado 1980, pp. 124–5)

Summary of the Hellenistic paradigm

Context
Delay of the parousia, failure of Christ to return.
Influence of Platonic philosophy on Christianity (rise of Gnosticism).
Spread of the Church throughout the Greek-speaking towns of the Roman empire.

Hierarchy of authorities
1. Reason: Platonic philosophy
2. Tradition: Nicaean Orthodoxy
3. Scripture (often interpreted allegorically)

Methodology for theology
Apologetics: interpreting and presenting Christianity through the categories of Platonism.

Eschatology
Eternal life is knowledge of God: the liturgy allows the believer to gain this knowledge of head and heart and ascend to union with God (*theosis*).

Christology
Incarnational: Christ the divine *logos*, the Word or principle of God found in all things, whom Jesus reveals in his life, death and resurrection.

Discipleship
To become a pupil of divine knowledge, prepared for baptism through the catechumenate and brought to union with God in the liturgy throughout adult life.

Mission of the Church
To celebrate the liturgy as widely as possible so that the divine light of truth shines through it into every community and draws all people into union with God.

Ministry
To enact the liturgy of the Church so that the whole community might see and know the divine light and love of eternal knowledge.

Some recent examples
Orthodox churches all around the world; the theology of Michael Ramsey; Taizé.

Debate

How far does this type of mission express the principles demonstrated by Jesus in his ministry?

Galilean principles of the *missio Christi* (from p. 33)

1. Contemplative listening, which frames all ministry: listening to God, to other people, to oneself, especially in times of prayer and retreat.

2. Addressing society as a whole, at points where people live and work, including and especially the marginalized. This results in being received and accepted by some but rejected and opposed by others.

3. Pointing to the inaugurated yet still awaited kingdom, in word and in surprising saving deed (symbolic actions) which address the actual needs of people (both individual and structural); but without publicizing the wonders.

4. Calling for a personal response by all to the coming of this kingdom.

5. Doing all this through a collaborative team, who themselves are powerless and vulnerable and must suffer the consequences.

One response

It is clear from the above, especially in the study of Antony of Egypt and the birth of monasticism, that the Hellenistic paradigm gave an important place to contemplation, cultivating the virtues of stillness and openness to the divine. The monastic movement provided ongoing expression for this over the centuries. Modern renewal movements such as the Taizé community and its followers have given this dimension of Christian living a remarkable contemporary expression. The first Galilean principle, then, can be found within this paradigm and mission type.

We have also seen the way the Hellenistic Church did not draw sharp boundaries between the Christian community and the wider society but identified itself fundamentally with the whole community: the point of mission was to draw the whole community to the liturgy, to the iconostasis, to the opening of the gateway between heaven and earth which would allow those two realms to meet and be reconciled. The second Galilean principle, then, also finds expression. But Hellenistic mission was centripetal rather than centrifugal, waiting for the people to be drawn into worship rather than going out to find people in their own homes and places of work. This aspect of Jesus' mission does not find such strong expression in this paradigm. (It is important to note, however, Brother Roger and the Taizé community were aware of the need to go out in this way: part of their witness has been for brothers to live in poor communities around the world.)

With regard to the fourth principle, the Hellenistic emphasis on right belief ('orthodoxy') shows an awareness of the importance of a personal response by the believer. It is not enough to attend the liturgy: participation must include an interior *theosis* as the human and divine meet in communion. Bosch describes John 3.16, with its emphasis on a person's belief in the Son as the key to their eternal life, as the text that best epitomizes the Orthodox understanding of mission. And, within this tradition, love is expressed in *kenosis*, an 'inner, voluntary self-denial which makes room to receive and embrace the other to whom it turns' (Bosch 1991, p. 208).

With reference to the fifth principle and the importance of collaboration in mission, the association of mission with the corporate life of the whole Church and with ordinary people 'gossiping the gospel', as seen above, shows a collective ownership of what was going on. This collaborative approach to ministry was highlighted by Bevans and Schroeder, who described the evangelists, bishops and teachers as supplementing rather than dominating what was going on (at least before 312). The Hellenistic type scores highly here (though after Constantine's founding of Christendom, as we shall see, clericalization began to develop in the East as well as the West).

It is with reference to the third Galilean principle that some serious questions arise. The Hellenistic type points to the presence of the kingdom within the world, an eternal realm that anyone can access through divine knowledge. It does not see this realm as lying in the future and coming through change and struggle. It therefore entails a certain acceptance of the social and political *status quo* and a loss of the radical and transformatory dimension of Jesus' mission. The Hellenistic Church, and its Orthodox progeny, has been attacked by some in the West along these lines. Bosch clearly summarizes the criticism:

> Platonic categories of thought all but destroyed primitive Christian eschatology . . . The church established itself in the world as an institute of almost exclusively other-worldly salvation. Faith in the promises of Christ still to be fulfilled tended to make room for faith in Christ's already accomplished eternal reign, which could henceforth be experienced and manifested only in the cultic-sacramental context of the liturgy. The apocalyptic gospel, which had fervently anticipated God's intervention in history, was replaced by a timeless gospel according to which the delay of the parousia made no vital difference. The element of urgency and crisis was wiped out by the idea of gradually drawing nearer to perfection, through various 'pedagogical' phases. Taking their cue from the incarnation of Christ, theologians such as Irenaeus, Clement of Alexandria and Origen described the believer's ascent from the moment of rebirth, through stages, up to the final point where he or she sees God . . . When all is said and done, this world and its history are not real; it is illusory. (Bosch 1991, p. 213)

Discussion questions

Are there local contexts, such as in drab and ugly urban areas, where this type of mission may nevertheless be just what is needed?
What might the strengths and weaknesses of this type of mission be within your own local context?

Further reading

Allchin, A. M. (1995), 'Michael Ramsey and the Orthodox Tradition', in Robin Gill and Lorna Kendall, eds., *Michael Ramsey as Theologian*, DLT

Balado, J. L. G. (1980), *The Story of Taizé*, Mowbray

Bevans, Stephen B., and Roger P. Schroeder (2004), *Constants in Context: A Theology of Mission for Today*, Orbis

Bosch, David J. (1991), *Transforming Mission: Paradigm Shifts in Theology of Mission*, Orbis

Bradley, Ian (2000), *Colonies of Heaven: Celtic Models for Today's Church*, DLT

Chadwick, Owen (1990), *Michael Ramsey: A Life*, Oxford University Press

Charlesworth, Max (2002), *Philosophy and Religion: From Plato to Postmodernism*, Oneworld

Cunningham, Mary (2002), *Faith in the Byzantine World*, Lion

Earey, Mark, and Carolyn Headley (2002), *Mission and Liturgical Worship*, Grove Books

Frend, W. H. C. (1984), *The Rise of Christianity*, DLT

Hill, Jonathan (2003), *The History of Christian Thought*, Lion

Miles, Margaret (2005), *The Word Made Flesh: A History of Christian Thought*, Blackwell

Olsen, Ted (2003), *Christianity and the Celts*, Lion

Pagels, Elaine (2006), *The Gnostic Gospels*, new edition, Phoenix Press

Ramsey, Michael (1964), *Canterbury Essays and Addresses*, SPCK

Ramsey, Michael (1972), *The Christian Priest Today*, SPCK

Senior, D., and C. Stuhlmueller (1983), *The Biblical Foundation of Mission*, Orbis

Stevenson, J., and W. H. C. Frend (1987), *The New Eusebius: Documents Illustrating the History of the Church to AD 336*, SPCK

Ware, Timothy (1963), *The Orthodox Church*, Penguin

Ware, Bishop Kallistos (1979), *The Orthodox Way*, Mowbray

7

Establishing Christendom Medieval Catholic Mission

In one of the state rooms in the Vatican hangs a magnificent painting by Federico Zuccaro (*c.*1540–1609) commissioned by the Counter-Reformation papacy to commemorate a moment of high drama and huge significance in the history of Christianity. It depicts the meeting of two great figures, the most powerful king of his time, King Henry IV of the Holy Roman Empire (which ranged over the German states of central Europe and the northern half of Italy, as far south as Rome) and Pope Gregory VII, also known as Hildebrand, who by reigning over the Roman Catholic Church controlled the single most powerful network of economic, intellectual and political influence in Western Europe. Now that the threat of Viking, Muslim and Hun invaders had receded, the kingdoms of Europe were beginning to stabilize and establish their own power base. But who was to be dominant: king or pope? Which institution was to inherit the mantle of the Emperor Constantine and be the supreme authority in the West: monarchy or papacy? The painting by Zuccaro gives a clear and definitive answer, for in the painting Henry IV is depicted as wearing penitential garb and bowing in submission before Gregory VII. The pope is depicted as seated and raised above the king, calmly and authoritatively giving absolution to the wretched monarch. The reasons for this amazing *coup* at the summit of the medieval hierarchy will be explored later in this chapter, but for now it is simply necessary to note how the event depicted in the painting represents the triumph of a new and hugely influential paradigm of Christian life and mission. (The painting is reproduced in Woodhead 2004, p. 114.)

Küng and Bosch describe this paradigm as holding sway over the Western

Church from the papacy of Gregory the Great (590–604) until the eve of the age of discovery (1492) and they argue that it has continued to be influential in parts of the Roman Catholic Church since then. So it begins in the period following the collapse of the Roman empire, traditionally described as the dark ages in the West but one of deep creativity in certain centres of learning across the continent. It starts at a time when pagan religion was still widespread, and it ends at a point when the whole continent was indisputably Christian but was about to fragment through the Reformation. While this period had many diverse currents and cross-currents influencing religious life, and while the Hellenistic paradigm continued to be influential in many quarters, over the period as a whole a distinctive form of Christian life and thought is observable with its own influential mission type. It is this that Küng and Bosch have pointed to and that this chapter explores and debates.

Background

The impact of the Emperor Constantine (d.337)

The roots of the new paradigm lie in the fourth century, in the Hellenistic age. They lie with a vision that the young Emperor Constantine saw on the night before his army fought for supremacy over the Western empire against his brother Maxentius at the Milvian Bridge near Rome. It is reported by a contemporary writer that Constantine 'was directed in a dream to mark the heavenly sign of God on the shields of his soldiers and thus to join battle. He did as he was ordered and with the cross-shaped letter X, with its top bent over, he marked Christ on the shields. Armed with this sign his army engaged the enemy and was completely victorious' (Stevenson and Frend 1987, p. 283).

Constantine may have been encouraged to place himself in the service of the Christian God because of the rapid spread of Christianity through the Roman empire: he would do himself no harm in gaining the support of an increasingly significant section of the population. At any rate this was a momentous turning point for the faith, gaining support from the imperial rulers for the first time.

As Constantine took control of the Western empire he stopped persecution of the Church and, in the Edict of Milan of 313, allowed Christians to have legal ownership of their churches. His family and court began to adopt the faith in increasing numbers. Then in 324 he marched east to fight his other brother Licinius for control of the eastern half of the Roman empire. At a battle near the Bosphorus Constantine was victorious and became the undisputed head of the whole Roman empire. He decided to build a new city on the banks of the Bosphorus and to name it after himself: Constantinople. It would become the new capital.

As Constantine settled in the east he found the Greek churches bitterly divided between Bishop Alexander of Alexandria and his presbyter Arius over a theological dispute concerning the nature of Christ. Constantine could not tolerate his power base, the Christian Church, being divided in this way. So he called a meeting of all the bishops at his summer residence at Nicaea, a few miles from Constantinople, in 325. The council reached agreement on a creed (218 out of 220 bishops signing the creed). The presence of the emperor's own troops outside the meeting may have helped to concentrate the minds of the bishops. Other new laws were passed which began to introduce a whole new way of governing and thinking about the Church. There were twenty canons regulating church discipline: bishops were not allowed to move from one diocese to another, they had to be consecrated by all the bishops of their province if possible and by not fewer than three, and the bishops of the provincial capitals (metropolitans) were given the right of veto. All of this helped to establish a clear structure within the hierarchy of the Church, and also centralized power in the hands of the bishops. Three bishops, of Rome, Alexandria and Antioch, were recognized as having a wider authority (Constantinople would soon be added to this list).

> The Nicene canons throw much light, therefore, on the developing organization and 'power structure' of the church. By 325 the Greek churches at least were accustomed to an organization based on the secular provincial system, and the unit normally conformed to that of the State. But what court of appeal could stand above a provincial council? . . . In fact, as the fourth century advanced, it became increasingly the tendency for the final decisions about church policy to be taken by the emperor, and the group in the church which at any given time swayed the course of events was very often that which succeeded in obtaining the imperial ear. (Chadwick 1967, pp. 131–2)

The Church, then, was becoming the religious arm of the Roman government. All of this shows the birth of 'Christendom', with the Christian community firmly embedded within the political structure, in a position of power and wealth, but under a Christian monarch who has authority over the Church as well as the state.

Eusebius, a contemporary Christian historian and a great admirer of Constantine, eulogized the emperor in an address delivered towards the end of his reign in 336:

> The only begotten Word of God reigns, from ages which had no beginning, to infinite and endless ages, the partner of his Father's kingdom. And our emperor ever beloved by him, who derives the source of imperial authority from above, and is strong in the power of his sacred title, has controlled the empire of the world for a long period of years. (Stevenson and Frend 1987, p. 367)

This statement shows that while the emperor was no longer regarded as being a god he was nevertheless seen by some in the Church as having significant divine authority. It is a statement that demonstrates how far the Church itself had travelled in its self-understanding. Eusebius then goes on to describe the missionary implications of this imperial theology:

> Again, that Preserver of the universe orders the whole heaven and earth, and the celestial kingdom, consistently with his Father's will. Even so our emperor whom He loves, by bringing those whom he rules on earth to the only begotten and saving Word renders them fit subjects for his kingdom. (ibid.)

Here, then, the emperor was being given a mandate to use the power of the empire to bring its diverse peoples into the Christian religion: the use of coercion within mission was being sanctioned. While Constantine himself allowed a plurality of religions to be practised in the empire, a later emperor, Theodosius, would do as Eusebius suggests and in 380 proscribe all religions except Christianity.

All of this throws sharp light on the statement in the Nicene creed (which was formally adopted at the Council of Constantinople of 381), which describes the Church as 'one' as well as 'holy', 'catholic' and 'apostolic'. The Church was to be *one* as the Roman empire was *one*, exercising authority over everyone within the empire. The Christendom paradigm, in other words, had made an initial appearance on the world stage: there was to be one order, with Christ at the head and beneath him the emperor (or, later, the pope) exercising a magisterial authority over the peoples of the earth. Implicit within this was a new understanding of mission: the Church was to come into an increasing unity with the state and together do all they could to incorporate more and more people within its jurisdiction. The Church, in other words, was to work for *the establishing of Christendom.*

In the Eastern empire this marriage of church and state remained as the norm for the next thousand years. The emperor's authority was supreme, under God. The Patriarch of Constantinople, appointed by the emperor, came to be seen as the most senior of the Eastern patriarchs but had to do as he was bid by the emperor. The episcopal seat, in the great basilica of Saint Sophia, was next door to the emperor's throne in the imperial palace, and under its authority.

Augustine of Hippo in the medieval West

In the Western empire the picture became more confused. The invasion of Alaric and the Goth hordes, with the sacking of Rome in 410, was a dramatic sign of the collapse of the empire and its ordered way of life. It might also have signified the collapse of the Western Church which had become so tied to the affairs of the empire. But St Augustine of Hippo (354–430), writing in Latin and one of the greatest of Western theologians, established a theological framework that would give the Church a renewed sense of its own inherent authority in the medieval world.

Two influential themes of this theology were forged in two separate controversies, one with a British monk called Pelagius and the other with the Donatist movement of North Africa. These two controversies made Augustine develop his understanding of how the Christian gains access to the kingdom of heaven, and this had important implications for mission.

1. Pelagius believed that it is possible for human beings to take their own initial steps towards salvation: by their own efforts they could turn and move towards divine grace. Augustine, based on his reading of Paul in Galatians and Romans, became increasingly convinced of the deep corruption and sinfulness of humankind and of its inability to raise itself up. He saw his own life as one of sincere but futile attempts to find salvation: 'My inner self was a house divided

against itself' (*Confessions* VIII.8). He developed the doctrine of original sin to account for this weakness, coming to see sex as the mechanism through which it is passed from generation to generation. All of this implied that the upward pedagogical process leading to *theosis*, found in the Hellenistic theologians, was also suspect.

Augustine saw that salvation must be entirely the gift of God. Learning from Paul's teaching on justification, he saw that our sinful condition

> is so perilous that only God can change it, without any contribution from us. We are, in this, totally powerless, delivered into Satan's hands, until we are ransomed from his dominion. Since our dilemma is a human one, only a human can satisfy God's demands in this respect; but since all human beings are themselves sinners, only somebody who is sinless and both human and divine can meet this condition and satisfy God vicariously on behalf of other human beings. This is in fact what Christ did, through his vicarious death on the cross. It happened once for all, and now holds true objectively; all that remains is for individuals to appropriate this salvation subjectively . . . (Bosch 1991, p. 216)

This shows how Augustine's theology brought the cross to the centre of the faith: it was Christ's death on the cross that achieved salvation for the believer, not their own efforts. It also shows how God must be the one who decides who shall be saved and who will not, because only he has the power to effect such an outcome. The doctrine of predestination, then, is implied by this theology of divine sovereignty and grace and became Augustine's direct response to Pelagius: we are not free to move towards salvation; it is God who moves towards us, having predestined some to be saved and others not to be saved. Those to be saved belong to the city of God; the rest belong to the earthly city; in this life both cities are intermingled but in the next life they will be separated (Stevenson and Frend 1989, p. 229).

All of this is significant for mission because it places the individual soul at the centre of mission: to belong to a corporate community that has access to the gate of heaven, as in the Hellenistic paradigm, is not enough. The issue is whether the individual person has appropriated that fact for themselves. The community as a whole, through teaching or liturgy, cannot do this on their behalf: justification through the cross of Christ can only be appropriated by the individual believer. Bosch describes this as the individualization of salvation and it would have dramatic effects on the practice of Christian mission, especially during the Reformation era.

2. The other great controversy would have a greater impact in the medieval period. This was with the Donatist movement in North Africa, which had been founded by Christians who had suffered persecution under the Emperor Diocletian and had then been outraged when, on the accession of Constantine, some of their persecutors had joined the Church and been promoted through the hierarchy. One of them had helped to consecrate the new bishop of Carthage in 311, and this had led to Donatus and his followers walking out and forming their own church. They were sincere and orthodox Christians who believed the Church should exclude any who committed gross sins. They believed the Church should be quite separate from the state. It was a widespread and popular movement in North Africa in the fourth and fifth centuries.

Augustine did not deny that the Church contained many who were 'drunkards, misers, tricksters, gamblers, adulterers, fornicators . . .' But he believed that every Christian, as we have seen, was embroiled in a sinful life and far from righteous. He thought the self-righteousness of the Donatists might be worse than most. The great sin, though, is separation from the one Catholic Church, because it had been founded by the apostles and was the only true Church, so that those who left it were severing their relationship with God. He recalled Cyprian's statement, *extra ecclesiam nulla salus* ('there is no salvation outside the Church') and used it to condemn the separation of the Donatists. Augustine insisted that visible unity and salvation went hand in hand. He urged them to come back to the Catholic Church:

> For what truth is there in the profession of the charity of Christ by him who does not embrace his unity? When, therefore, [the Donatists] come to the Catholic Church, they gain thereby not what they had already possessed, but something which they had not before – namely, that those things which they possessed begin then to be profitable to them. For in the Catholic Church they obtain the root of charity in the bond of peace and in the fellowship of unity; so that all the sacraments of truth which they have serve not for condemnation, but for liberation. (Stevenson and Frend 1989, pp. 218–19)

This meant that the moral and theological standing of bishops or laity was irrelevant to the authority and holiness of the Church. Its claims were based on its foundation by the apostles and it was imperative that Christians participated in its sacraments, teaching and discipline. Bosch describes this as 'the ecclesiasticization of salvation' (1991, p. 217).

In his great but disorderly work, *City of God*, Augustine described how this incorporation into the Church was for the Christian also an incorporation into citizenship of God's city, an eternal city that would never be extinguished by the barbarian hordes. While the Christian lived alongside those who belonged to the other city, the earthly city, which *would* be extinguished, they also belonged to God's reign that would last for all eternity (Bosch 1991, pp. 220–1). It is important to add, though, that Augustine did not identify the Catholic Church with the city of God: the two were distinct in his thinking. As the centuries passed, however, the two came increasingly to be seen as one, with entry into one being regarded as entry into the other (ibid., p. 221).

Mission within the medieval Catholic paradigm

The theology of Augustine had profound implications for mission in the medieval era, which began with the sack of Rome and lasted until the Renaissance. It undermined the Hellenistic mission type in a fundamental way. It showed, as we have seen, that mission could not primarily be the lifting of a whole community through teaching and liturgy into eternal truth. Human sin was so pervasive that this would never be possible. Salvation was entirely the gift of God through the cross of Christ to certain people, the elect, to be appropriated by them with gratitude and humility.

Yet, for Augustine, the Church was indispensable because this gift was given through the Church: only membership of the Church could allow salvation to be imparted to a believer, for salvation depended on unity with the Church of the apostles. Mission, then, was to be all about bringing as many people as possible into sacramental membership of the Church so that they could then receive the salvation wrought by Christ and become citizens of the city of God.

This meant that an awareness of boundaries *between* people came back into mission theology: Augustine's theology created a sharp and decisive boundary between those who were part of the sacramental life of the Church and those who were not, and mission was all about moving them across this boundary.

Furthermore, as we have seen, this theology was developed within the context of the rise of Christendom, with the Emperor Constantine and his successors assuming a governing role over the Church and bringing the Church within the arms of the imperial state. This meant that the Church was now a privileged organization and that the state would enforce its will. It did not take long before this started to happen, with the Catholic Church using the imperial state to further its missionary work, and appealing to Jesus' parable of the great banquet, where the householder instructs his servants to 'Compel them to come in' (Luke 14.23), as justification for such coercion.

Augustine's struggle with the Donatists provides an early example, with Augustine advising the Roman official Marcellinus on how to (moderately) punish Donatists:

> Fulfil, Christian judge, the duty of an affectionate father; let your indignation against their crimes be tempered by consideration of humanity; do not be provoked by the atrocity of their sinful deeds to gratify the passion of revenge, but rather bring your will to bear so as to cure the wounds of sinners. (Stevenson and Frend 1989, p. 226)

Rather than torture the Donatist sectarians Augustine recommends the use of beating with rods as a fitting punishment (p. 227).

This association of a church-centred mission with coercion was to gain strength over the course of the Middle Ages. The advice of Pope Gregory the Great to landowners in Sardinia, on how to compel their peasant workers to be baptized, is a more extreme example: Gregory suggested that the peasants were to be '"so burdened with rent that the weight of this punitive exaction should make them hasten to righteousness". Those who would not listen to reason, if they were slaves, were "to be chastised by beating and torture, whereby they might be brought to amendment". Free men were to be jailed. All of this, of course, was for the non-believers' own good' (Bosch 1991, pp. 222–3). When it came to Jews, however, Gregory demonstrated a scrupulous concern for justice and humanity (ibid., pp. 225–6).

The association of the Western Church with secular power reached a defining moment in the year 800. This was when Pope Leo III crowned the Frankish king Charlemagne as emperor of a huge swathe of European territory (the largest area to be ruled by one ruler since the fall of the Western Roman empire). Charlemagne had written to Leo that as emperor his task was to defend the holy Church of Christ everywhere against the assaults of pagans and the ravages of unbelievers. The pope's responsibility, like that of Moses, was to intercede for the emperor and his military campaigns, 'so that, through your intercession and God's guidance and grace, the Christian people may always and everywhere be victorious over the enemies of Christ's name' (ibid., p. 221). This shows how each needed the other: Leo brought a spiritual legitimacy to Charlemagne's rule: Charlemagne protected and supported Leo.

But who was to have the supreme authority, church or state, pope or king? Under Constantine there had been no question: the emperor had authority over church as well as state. But now that the Western Roman empire had collapsed the field was again open. Charlemagne had instructed Leo to crown him, and so in secular terms was showing his supremacy. But to receive Leo's spiritual blessing through the coronation was a sign of his need to receive the authority that Leo could give. Some ambiguity was therefore part of the relationship. But when Hildebrand became Pope Gregory VII in 1073, he was determined there should be no ambiguity.

Case study: Pope Gregory VII and Roman supremacy

Hildebrand was a monk of obscure origins who became very active as a papal legate at a time when the Roman Church was seeking to carve out its own power base between the rival courts of the Normans (also called Franks) and the German kings (the successors of Charlemagne). It was the Germans who controlled much of Italy and had previously nominated the popes. The papacy was seeking to secure the right to make its own appointment of bishops and church officials across the continent, and to enforce clerical celibacy. Hildebrand is a controversial figure who has been described as 'a man of rare honesty, without fear, impatient and unscrupulous, he could be rough even to his friends and even more cruel to his enemies' (Küng 1995, p. 380). He was probably behind the papal invitation to the Normans in 1059 to take control of southern Italy and Sicily from the German kings.

When the previous pope died in 1073, with the funeral rites still in progress, he was elected as the new pope to tumultuous acclaim but with a blatant failure to follow the correct procedure for elections. He named himself Gregory VII, after Gregory the Great, showing his intention to be a strong pope, and set about enhancing the authority of the papacy within the power struggles of Europe.

There are two powerful examples of this. The first is his formulation of the 'Dictatus Papae', a document describing 27 principles of papal primacy. They may have been formulated as chapter headings of a planned collection of laws. More than any other document of the time, these 'Dictates' demonstrate Gregory's belief in papal supremacy not only over the Church but over the courts of Europe. Some examples are as follows:

1 The Roman Church has been founded only by the Lord.
2 Only the Bishop of Rome is legitimately called universal bishop.
3 He alone can depose or reinstate bishops.
7 He alone is permitted, if the age requires it, to decree new laws, establish new bishoprics, transform chapters of canons into monasteries and vice versa, divide rich sees and combine poor ones.
8 He alone may use imperial insignia.
9 All rulers have to kiss only the Pope's feet.
12 He is permitted to depose emperors.
17 No legal statement and no book may be regarded as canonical without his authorization.
22 The Roman see has never erred, and according to the testimony of Scripture will never err.
23 The Roman pontiff, if he has been consecrated canonically, is beyond doubt sanctified through the merits of St Peter . . . (Küng 1995, p. 380)

These principles show an almost mystical identification with St Peter and explain Gregory VII's belief that he had unlimited competence over ordination, legislation, administration and jurisdiction. They also explain his subsequent struggle with the German king, to which we now turn.

This was the investiture dispute with the German King Henry IV. It concerned the right of appointing bishops within the German territories: was the king or the pope to make the appointments? At the Lent Synod in 1075 Gregory renewed a prohibition on lay people making clerical appointments, which implied that Henry had no right to make appointments. Henry took no notice and continued to appoint his own people to Italian bishoprics such as that of Milan. In December 1075 Gregory sent an ultimatum to the king threatening him with excommunication 'and the fate of Saul' if he continued with the nomination of bishops. At an imperial meeting in 1076 Henry reacted by formally deposing the pope: Hildebrand, he declared, was no longer Pope but a false monk. A few weeks later at the Lent Synod in Rome, Gregory responded by excommunicating and 'deposing' the king, suspending all those bishops who had supported the king and releasing all Henry's subjects from their oath of loyalty to him. This may seem ambitious, but Gregory knew his audience and that many of Europe's princes and bishops did not support Henry. And the latter, a young and inexperienced king, slowly realized that he must submit to the pope. They met at the fortress of Canossa and here, bare-footed and in penitential garb, the king appeared before the castle gate on 25 January 1077, asking for pardon. After an unprecedented three days of penance, and only after the pleading of his host and others, 'the Pope, having forced Henry to prostrate himself on the ground in the form of a cross, graciously raised him up and released him from the ban. In this way, while Henry's royal status was restored, it was at the same time stripped of its sacral character and its ideological basis was shaken: Canossa was the turning point!' (Küng 1995, p. 386).

Some years later (in 1084), however, Gregory had to flee Rome when Henry arrived at the city with an army. He turned to the Normans for help, which they provided, but at the cost of harshly sacking Rome. These events, though, did not diminish the huge impact of the encounter at Canossa on European thinking: this encounter showed that the papacy was a force to be reckoned with, not just spiritually but temporally, and it established the powerful actuality of a distinctive Roman Catholic mission type:

> What had hitherto been merely programmatic and an idea, was to be made concrete in the world at large. The papacy under his intrepid direction was propelled by its own inner strength and programme to become an institution of European dimensions. The papacy had made Hildebrand, and Gregory VII was to make it the focal establishment of Europe. The fifth century view that the Roman church was the mother of all churches from now on began to approach reality, though at the time she was a harsh mother and the pope a monarchic ruler and exacting father. (Walter Ullmann, in Küng 1995, p. 381)

The French theologian Yves Congar sums up Gregory's impact in the following terms: 'To obey God means to obey the church and that in turn means to obey the Pope, and vice versa.' He is the pope who makes the pre-eminence of the see of Peter, the Roman church, 'the axis of all ecclesiology' (ibid., p. 381). For Küng, Gregory is the pope 'who radically and irrevocably put the Roman Catholic paradigm of the Middle Ages into political practice' (ibid., p. 380). So while the struggle for supremacy by pope over princes would continue throughout the Middle Ages (such as in the story of St Thomas Becket, and in the words of Pope Boniface VIII in his Bull of 1302, *Unam Sanctam*: 'We declare, state, define, and proclaim that it is altogether necessary to salvation for every human creature to be subject to the Roman pontiff'), the life and dictates of Gregory VII provide the classical expression of this type (see Figure 5).

Medieval Catholicism developed in at least two significant directions, neither of which we have space to explore. One was through the use of military coercion to force peoples into baptism and membership of the Church. There are a number of examples, from Charlemagne's subjugation of the Saxons, to

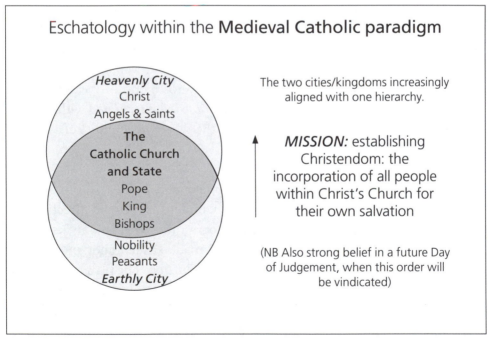

Figure 5

Olav Tryggvason's violent Christianization of Norway in the late tenth century. But these remained the exception. The Crusades might be thought to provide another example, but, as Bosch points out, they were not launched to *convert* the Muslims but to defeat and overwhelm them, and so cannot be seen as a direct expression of Christian mission (Bosch 1991, p. 225).

The other significant development was the spread of monasticism throughout the Middle Ages. We have already examined the origins of monasticism in the life of St Antony and seen that this reformed and renewed the Hellenistic Christian paradigm. Monasticism began as one way in which human and divine could find union, in this case through living in the desert and fighting the forces of evil in those places away from the distractions and temptations of urban life. In the West, through Celtic monasticism and through Benedict, the founder of Western monasticism (480–547), this remained the controlling paradigm: the Christian life of the monk was to serve the magnifying of God's name and to be all about the 'ascent to God' through twelve successive 'degrees of humility', so that the monk arrives 'at the love of God which, being perfect, casts out fear'. Inspired by his rule the Benedictine movement created monasteries which became 'a school for the Lord's service', and did so for six centuries. These monasteries became the model on which all others were designed and have continued to exercise a profound influence: 'Seeking a life free from corruption and free from distraction in its daily worship, in which each day, each hour, would have its own completeness' (Bosch 1991, p. 234). Running through all this is a translation of Antony's monasticism into a Western setting and, with it, a recurring expression of the Hellenistic Christian paradigm.

Monasticism, however, also came to be influenced by the medieval Catholic paradigm. This is seen in the commissioning of the monk Augustine (of Canterbury) by Gregory the Great for a missionary journey to England to establish the Catholic Church and to bring its people into the fold. Even though Celtic monastic houses and churches were well established in many parts of the British Isles, this was not deemed sufficient by Gregory: a union between the British and the see of Peter must be established. Augustine was the first of a number of remarkable missionaries who spread Catholic faith and discipline across Western Europe: Boniface of Crediton 'the apostle of Germany', Willibrord and Alcuin of York being other examples (Bosch 1991, p. 235). In all of this work monasticism showed that it could be influenced by and become the expression of the medieval Catholic paradigm in the sense that its goal became the spread and consolidation of the Augustinian and papal Christianity seen above. The same could be said of the mendicant Christianity of the later Middle Ages, as represented by the Franciscans and the Dominicans. Francis of Assisi, after all, at the start of his extraordinary ministry, had been inspired by his contemplation of a crucifix through which the Lord had told him to 'rebuild my Church'. He had then sought the Pope's validation of his order and rule (see Bevans and Schroeder 2004, ch. 5).

Some other expressions of the type

The establishing of Christendom, a union of church and state, has continued to be an influential mission type since the Middle Ages. It has not been restricted to the Roman Catholic tradition but has been influential within some Protestant traditions as well. In these cases, while the pope has not been recognized as supreme, the notion that church and state work hand in hand in governing the life of the nation has been present. Martin Luther, who in other respects presented a very different type (as we shall see in the next chapter), laid the groundwork for this continuity when he called on the German nobility to assist the objectives of the Reformation (for example in his famous pamphlet of 1520, *An Appeal to the Christian Nobility*). The forming of 'Magisterial Protestantism', where the local secular magistrate (a king or a prince or a local official) is regarded as having authority over the affairs of the Church, derives from Luther's teaching.

The establishment of the Church of England

A good example is found in the 'Articles of Religion' and certain prayers within *The Book of Common Prayer* of the Church of England, originally compiled by Thomas Cranmer (1489–1556), the Archbishop of Canterbury in the reigns of Henry VIII and Edward VI. Cranmer was a follower of Luther in these matters (though on other theological issues closer to the Reformed tradition of Zwingli and Calvin) and presents an Anglican version of the Christendom type. The Articles of Religion were originally 42 Articles and appeared in 1553 in the reign of Henry VIII. They were reduced to 39 ten years later and were issued in their present form in 1571 under Elizabeth I. Paul Avis explains what kind of text they are: 'A cursory glance at the Articles will show that they are not a complete account of Christian doctrine, even less an Anglican systematic theology. They are in fact a response to matters of controversy in the sixteenth century. They make certain central affirmations directed against several specific targets: anti-trinitarianism, Roman Catholicism and radical Protestantism' (Avis 2000, p. 52).

Article XXXVII turns into a significant statement of the establishment type:

> The King's Majesty hath the chief power in this Realm of England, and other his Dominions, unto whom the chief Government of all Estates of this Realm, whether they be Ecclesiastical or Civil, in all causes doth appertain, and is not, nor ought to be, subject to any foreign Jurisdiction.
>
> Where we attribute to the King's Majesty the chief government, by which Titles we understand the minds of some slanderous folks to be offended; we give not to our Princes the ministering either of God's Word, or of the Sacraments, the which thing the Injunctions also lately set forth by Elizabeth our Queen do most plainly testify; but that only prerogative, which we see to have been given always to all godly Princes in holy Scriptures by God himself; that is, that they should rule all estates and degrees committed to their charge by God, whether they be Ecclesiastical or Temporal, and restrain with the civil sword the stubborn and evil-doers.
>
> The Bishop of Rome hath no jurisdiction in this Realm of England.
>
> The Laws of the Realm may punish Christian men with death, for heinous and grievous offences.
>
> It is lawful for Christian men, at the commandment of the Magistrate, to wear weapons, and serve in the wars.

The monarch, then, is placed over the affairs of the Church as well as the state (though in line with Protestant theology he or she is restricted from having authority over preaching and sacramental worship). He or she takes the place of the pope in Gregory VII's outlook, and the pope is firmly banished from the kingdom. The monarch's authority is seen as coming from God through Scripture, and this authority includes the right to make Christian citizens take up arms on their behalf. Magisterial Protestantism as well as Papal Catholicism, then, envisages an almost total identification of church and state in the affairs of the world.

The Accession Service of *The Book of Common Prayer* presents another powerful statement of this divine sanctioning and upholding of Christendom. In this annual service, to be said on the anniversary of the monarch's accession to the throne, the Church is called to give to God 'unfeigned thanks' for setting the sovereign 'upon the throne of this Realm'. Then, in one of the collects, this sense of intimate union between God and monarch is reinforced:

> O God, who providest for thy people by thy power, and rulest over them in love; Vouchsafe so to bless thy Servant our Queen, that under her this nation may be wisely governed, and thy Church may serve thee in all godly quietness; and grant that she being devoted to thee with her whole heart, and persevering in good works unto the end, may by thy guidance, come to thy everlasting kingdom . . . (*Book of Common Prayer*, p. 599)

Christian mission, in this establishment Anglicanism, becomes the exercise of building up and maintaining the ordered state of the kingdom, with church and crown working together to this end. Ecclesiastical and temporal powers complement and reinforce each other, with the monarch set over both as 'supreme head' (in Henry VIII's phrase), or as 'supreme governor' (in the phrase of Elizabeth I and subsequent monarchs).

A picture of this approach is provided by the city of Lancaster in the north-west of England. On a hill in the centre of the city, overlooking the commercial centre, stands an austere castle. This is built on the site of a Roman fort and belongs to the monarch and is used as a prison (the Pendle witches were imprisoned here). Next door, with a tower that rises above the castle, stands the parish church of the city. From the town below, the castle and church appear to stand side by side, a picture of state and church in union with each other keeping watch and keeping order over the society below. If you walk into the church this impression of establishment is confirmed by the presence of a large military chapel with the flags of one of the Queen's regiments hanging from the ceiling in serried ranks. Most striking of all, above the pulpit, in clear view of the congregation, an impressive pulpit canopy hangs from a pillar and is surmounted by a symbolic carving: this shows a large Bible and, set upon it and *over it* in pride of place, the monarch's state crown.

Summary of the medieval Catholic paradigm

Context
Rise of Christendom from the Emperor Constantine onwards.
Augustine of Hippo's theology: the individualization and
ecclesiasticization of salvation.

Hierarchy of authorities
1. Tradition: the Catholicism of Augustine
2. Reason: an Aristotelian Platonism
3. Scripture as proof texts

Methodology for theology
Patriarchal: appealing to the early church fathers for validation of a
hierarchical Church and society.

Eschatology
The kingdom of heaven is closely identified with the Church.
Participation in the sacraments and discipline of the Church gains entry
into the kingdom. However, Christ the judge is also expected to come
with power at the end.

Christology
Redemptive: through his atoning death on the cross Christ has secured
redemption from death and hell for his elect.

Discipleship
To render obedience to crown and Church and to seek the redemption
of the cross through the sacraments of the Church, above all confession
('The Penitential Cycle' of the medieval Church).

Mission of the Church
To work with the state to bring as many people as possible into the
sacramental life of the Church so that they can participate in the
penitential cycle and receive salvation.

> **Ministry**
> A priestly ministry of promoting the sacraments, teaching and discipline of the Church within the laws of the state.
>
> **Some examples**
> Gregory VII; Magisterial Protestantism, e.g. establishment Anglicanism.

Debate

As with the other mission types, the mission of the medieval Catholic Church can be assessed against the principles that were identified in Jesus' ministry:

> ### Galilean principles of the *missio Christi* (from p. 33)
> 1. Contemplative listening, which frames all ministry: listening to God, to other people, to oneself, especially in times of prayer and retreat.
> 2. Addressing society as a whole, at points where people live and work, including and especially the marginalized. This results in being received and accepted by some but rejected and opposed by others.
> 3. Pointing to the inaugurated yet still awaited kingdom, in word and in surprising saving deed (symbolic actions) which address the actual needs of people (both individual and structural); but without publicizing the wonders.
> 4. Calling for a personal response by all to the coming of this kingdom.
> 5. Doing all this through a collaborative team, who themselves are powerless and vulnerable and must suffer the consequences.

One response

It would be hard to argue that the establishing of Christendom was framed by contemplative listening. As we have seen, medieval Catholic mission was closely associated with compulsion: the close ties between church and state, pope and king, that developed in the Middle Ages, with all the bloody consequences that followed, removed the possibility of the Church genuinely listening to those who were the subjects of its mission. The equation of salvation with membership of the Church undermined the need for genuine and open dialogue with those who did not belong to its institutional life.

However, when the monks started to support this type of mission, and especially when Francis of Assisi and the mendicant movement became a significant influence in the later Middle Ages, it is possible to argue that this principle was recovered in impressive ways. By travelling on foot, living in poverty and seeking literally to follow in the footsteps of Christ, this movement saw a return to many of the Galilean principles in Catholic mission. It is no accident that Francis went to the Muslim Turks of the Ottoman empire not to fight them but to engage them in dialogue.

This mission type fares better with the second Galilean principle. With the close connection between church and state, from Constantine onwards, came a close connection with the whole of the society over which the state presided. The Church became an institution with access to every corner of that society, having use of official communication networks and administration, and not just to those who chose to associate with it. The whole society could be addressed, and the results of this speak for themselves: at the beginning of the period some 5 per cent of the population of the Roman empire was Christian. By the end of the period the whole population of Europe was living and breathing a Christian culture.

Did the establishing of Christendom point to an inaugurated yet still awaited kingdom? Here there must again be serious questions. Constantine and his successors were keen to emphasize the established and fixed nature of the union between church, empire and eternal kingdom. The medieval Catholic paradigm was all about upholding and strengthening the *status quo*, whereas Jesus' message was that the kingdom was beginning to break in and overturn the current structures of the world. The radical and prophetic edge to his mission, emphasizing the imminence of upheaval, is clearly not part of this type. Neither king nor pope were interested in revolution: quite the opposite!

With the fourth principle, however, the picture is not so clear. Augustine's emphasis on the importance of the individual believer appropriating the salvation of Christ for themselves, through participation in the sacraments of the Church (and eventually the penitential cycle of the Middle Ages), was clearly creating the conditions for this principle to be expressed. But his acceptance of state coercion in the Donatist controversy, and the greater use of state coercion for Christian mission in the following centuries, was a sharp denial of the possibility of a personal response and negated a key aspect of the mission of Christ. Only in the later Middle Ages, with the rise of the mendicant movement, would there be the start of a renunciation of coercion within mission.

With the fifth principle, concerning collaboration, again it seems that it did not find expression in this mission type. The hierarchical authoritarianism of Christendom, whether based on emperor, pope or king, removed the possibility of genuine collaboration among the missionaries: they had to do what they were told even when, like Augustine of Canterbury, they were reluctant to do so.

Overall, then, this mission type does not seem to achieve an impressive score when assessed against the Galilean principles. It is significantly less successful than the preceding Hellenistic type. However, as already mentioned, it did regain some ground in the later Middle Ages.

It is important to note that some recent writers have defended the continuing establishment of church and state in Britain, notably Paul Avis, who cites the way an established church can reach every member of the society in which it is established. Avis argues that an established church is placed in a strong position for promoting mission in that society (see Avis 2001). It has also been defended from a Presbyterian Church of Scotland perspective by Ian Bradley, because of the way establishment allows the Church to exercise a pastoral and even prophetic ministry in every community of the land (see Bradley 2003). Lesslie Newbigin, no supporter of establishment in other circumstances, also wrote the following assessment, one which should make us hesitate before moving on to other mission types:

> Much has been written about the harm done to the cause of the gospel when Constantine accepted baptism, and it is not difficult to expatiate on this theme. But could any other choice have been made? When the ancient classical world . . . ran out of spiritual fuel and turned to the church as the one society that could hold a disintegrating world together, should the church have refused the appeal and washed its hands of responsibility for the political order? . . . It is easy to see with hindsight how quickly the church fell into the temptation of worldly power. It is easy to point . . . to the glaring contradiction between the Jesus of the Gospels and his followers occupying the seats of power and wealth. And yet we have to ask, would God's purpose . . .

have been better served if the church had refused all political responsibility? (*Foolishness to the Greeks*, WCC 1986, p. 100, quoted in Bosch 1991, p. 222)

Discussion questions

Are there contexts today, here or overseas, such as in lawless regions of Africa, where this type of mission may be appropriate to the needs of the moment?
How might this type of mission be expressed in your own local context?
What would its strengths and weaknesses be?

Further reading

Avis, Paul (2000), *The Anglican Understanding of the Church*, SPCK

Avis, Paul (2001), *Church, State and Establishment*, SPCK

Bevans, Stephen B., and Roger P. Schroeder (2004), *Constants in Context: A Theology of Mission for Today*, Orbis

Book of Common Prayer (1968), Standard edition, Cambridge University Press

Bosch, David J. (1991), *Transforming Mission: Paradigm Shifts in Theology of Mission*, Orbis

Bradley, Ian (2003), *God Save the Queen*, DLT

Chadwick, Henry (1967), *The Early Church*, Penguin

Evans, G. R. (2002), *Faith in the Medieval World*, Lion

Frend, W. H. C. (1984) *The Rise of Christianity*, DLT

Hill, Jonathan (2003), *The History of Christian Thought*, Lion

Küng, Hans (1995), *Christianity: Its Essence and History*, SCM Press

Miles, Margaret (2005), *The Word Made Flesh: A History of Christian Thought*, Blackwell

O'Donovan, O. M. T. and J. (1999), *From Irenaeus to Grotius*, Eerdmans

Southern, R. W. (1967), *The Making of the Middle Ages*, Hutchinson

Stevenson, J., and W. H. C. Frend (1987), *The New Eusebius: Documents Illustrating the History of the Church to AD 336*, SPCK

Stevenson, J., and W. H. C. Frend, (1989), *Creeds, Councils and Controversies: Documents Illustrating the History of the Church AD 337–461*, SPCK

Woodhead, Linda (2004), *An Introduction to Christianity*, Cambridge University Press

8

The Conversion of Souls Protestant Reformation Mission

There is a village 'delightfully lost in the Hodder valley above Clitherow [in Lancashire] where the Forest of Bowland descends towards Ribblesdale. The church sits proud on a mound, with a former village grammar school beyond it. The interior is notable for its 17th- and 18th-century woodwork, inserted after the stripping out of the pre-Reformation furnishings. Even the lime wash has survived . . .' (Jenkins 2000, p. 345). The church in question is St Andrew's, Slaidburn, and with these words Simon Jenkins sets the scene for an encounter with one of the most remarkable features of the building, its enormous three-decker pulpit. This is an ornate construction that catches the eye as soon as one enters the church. The first level was built for the parish clerk, to lead the responses to the minister's versicles in Mattins and Evensong. The second level was built for the minister to lead those services and read the Scriptures. The third level, at a great height above the congregation, was built for the preaching of the sermon. The altar, on the other hand, which in the original medieval church would have been an impressive stone construction and the focal point of the building, is now reduced to being a modest wooden table behind a wooden screen at the east end, out of sight to most of the congregation.

St Andrew's Church is a powerful example of the revolution that swept through English Christianity between the sixteenth and eighteenth centuries. It graphically illustrates how the sacramental Catholicism of the Middle Ages was replaced by a religion of the word, the word of Scripture and the word of the preacher endeavouring to reach into the souls of the assembled people. It shows the arrival of a new paradigm of Christian life and, within that, of a new type of mission. This is the subject of the following chapter.

Why did this revolution take place? An answer must begin in an Augustinian monk's cell in Germany.

Background

Augustine's awkward legacy

Augustine bequeathed a deep theological contradiction to the medieval world, one which helps to explain the eruption of the Reformation in the sixteenth century. On the one hand, arising out of his controversy with the Donatists, who argued that only worthy people could celebrate the sacraments and belong to the Church, he argued that the Church is a mixed community comprising bad as well as good. The parable of the tares, Augustine suggested, pointed to the mixed character of the Church as a historical institution. Only at the final consummation will the two groups be separated. So he promoted Cyprian's doctrine that *extra ecclesiam nulla salus* ('there is no salvation outside the Church'). This meant that as many people as possible must be compelled into baptism and the discipline of the Catholic Church, participating in what became the penitential cycle, for the sake of their own salvation.

But, on the other hand, Augustine also brought Paul's doctrine of justification by grace into the heart of Western Catholic theology. This described salvation as a freely given gift of God to the believer which could only be received by an inner conversion of the soul, a reception that only God could see. His belief in original sin and the utter dependence of the believer on God made him deny, in his controversy with Pelagius, the possibility of human freedom. And this led him to adopt the idea that God must have *predestined* those who are saved to be saved.

In his classic study of early Christian doctrine J. N. D. Kelly drew out the inherent contradiction between these two sets of beliefs:

Augustine came to make a significant admission in order to meet the Donatist's point that Christ's bride must be 'without spot or wrinkle' here and now. This consisted in drawing a careful distinction between the essential Church, composed of those who genuinely belong to Christ, and the outward or empirical Church . . . only those who are ablaze with charity and sincerely devoted to Christ's cause belong to the essential Church; the good alone 'are in a proper sense Christ's body' . . . The rest, that is to say sinners, may seem to be within the Church, but they have no part in 'the congregation and society of saints'; the 'holy Church' in the strict sense of the words. (Kelly 1977, pp. 415–16)

The error of the Donatists was to make a crude institutional division between them, whereas the precedent of Israel showed that the division was a spiritual one and that God intended the two types of people to exist side by side in this world.

As he worked out his doctrine of predestination, however, Augustine was led to introduce a refinement on this distinction between the visible and invisible Church. In the last resort, he came to see, the only true members of the Church (the 'enclosed garden . . . spring shut up, fountain sealed . . . the paradise with the fruit of apples' . . .) could be 'the fixed number of the elect'. But 'in God's ineffable foreknowledge many who seem to be within are without, and many who seem to be without are within'. In other words, many even of those who to all appearances belong to 'the invisible fellowship of love' may not possess the grace of perseverance, and are therefore destined to fall away; while many others who at present may be heretics or schismatics, or lead disordered lives or even are unconverted pagans, may be predestined to the fullness of grace. (ibid., p. 416)

Kelly points out that Augustine never attempted to harmonize this idea of the Church being a fixed number of the elect known only to God, with the idea that the essential Church is to be found within the institutional Catholic Church (though mixed up with sinners within that institution). '*Indeed, it may be doubted whether any synthesis was ultimately possible, for if the doctrine is taken seriously the notion of the institutional Church ceases to have any validity*' (ibid., pp. 416–17, italics mine).

The Reformation may be seen as the point when, finally, that doctrine was taken seriously and the visible institutional Church had to start surrendering its authority and power to the notion of the true Church as an invisible Church, of the elect known only to God.

How did this happen and what were its implications for mission?

Luther and justification by grace through faith

Martin Luther (1483–1546) is the pioneer of the Reformation paradigm of Christianity and, within that, of the Protestant Reformation type of mission. But he could not have made the impact that he did without a number of social, cultural and economic developments within western Europe. These include the development of new printing technology, the rise of the merchant class in the towns and cities of Europe and their increasing reluctance to pay taxes to Rome, the rise of humanist learning and its undermining of medieval scholasticism, and the papacy's increasing attempts to commercialize the business of religion which, in turn, fostered revulsion and opposition from many churchpeople.

The turning point, for Luther, was a spiritual and theological one. He began his adult life as an Augustinian monk, was highly committed to the religious life and was very serious about securing his eternal salvation through living a holy and righteous life. But he experienced an increasing sense of anguish and despair as he realized he was not succeeding in this. At the same time he was a university lecturer in Wittenberg who had recently studied some of Augustine's writings and was now engaged in lecturing on the Psalms and the epistles of Paul. He believed the epistle to the Romans was 'the most important document in the New Testament, the Gospel in its purest expression' (Miles 2005, p. 252). In later life he recounted how he studied and meditated on Romans 1.17 and 'the righteousness of God', sometime between 1516 and 1519:

> For my case was this: however irreproachable my life as a monk, I felt myself in the presence of God to be a sinner with a most unquiet conscience, nor could I believe him to be appeased by the satisfaction I could offer . . . I raged with a savage and confounded conscience . . . At last, as I meditated day and night, God showed mercy and I turned my attention to the connection of the words, namely – 'The righteousness of God is revealed, as it is written: the righteous shall live by faith' – and there I began to understand that the righteousness of God is the righteousness in which a just man lives by the gift of

God, in other words by faith, and that what Paul means is this: the righteousness of God, revealed in the Gospel, is *passive*, in other words that by which the merciful God justifies us through faith, as it is written, 'The righteous shall live by faith.' At this I felt myself straightway born afresh and to have entered through the open gates into paradise itself. There and then the whole face of scripture was changed . . . (from 'Autobiographical Fragment', March 1545, in McGrath 1999, pp. 106–10)

These words show that Luther's starting point was the hopelessness and futility of the human situation: he accepted fundamentally Augustine's doctrine of original sin and the dependence of humanity on God. Second, they show that he understood righteousness to be given to the believer as a gift, which is the grace of God. Third, that the response of the believer can only be passive, to simply accept the grace that God gives, rather than in any sense to actively seek it or earn it. Fourth, they show the sense of liberation and joy that this realization gave Luther: he now knew that the securing of salvation did not depend in any way on his own futile attempts to win it: it was already secured, by the death of Christ on the cross, and all he needed to do was trustingly receive it. This is the doctrine of justification by grace through faith: 'that the believer can be justified (declared righteous and therefore saved) only through faith (*per solam fidem*), by the merits of Christ imputed to him or her, with works or religious observance as irrelevant to this'. For Luther this doctrine became 'the centrepiece of our teaching' (Migliore 2005, p. 236).

There were a number of profound implications of this doctrine and Luther became more and more determined to follow them through and put them into practice: from a seemingly small theological insight came a whole new way of viewing the Christian faith, the life of the Church, and even the nature of Europe.

First, Luther followed Augustine in recognizing the subjective dimension of salvation: that the crucial arena for the receiving of salvation was within the soul of the believer and that what took place was known only to God. We have already seen this described by Bosch as 'the individualization of salvation', where the corporate life of the Church ceases to have a direct role in the securing of that salvation. Whereas Augustine remained committed to Cyprian's view of the necessity of the Church to salvation, for other reasons, Luther had no such commitments. He had already witnessed the corruption of the institutional Church, especially on his visit to Rome, and was outraged by the commercialization of religion through the selling of indulgences, and so had other reasons for downgrading the authority of the Church. The doctrine of justification by grace through faith, though, gave a theological rationale for sidelining the institutional Church in the salvation of the believer. The key relationship was between the individual believer and God, a direct and one-to-one engagement: everything else was secondary to this.

A second implication was the elevation of Scripture over the Church as the authoritative guide in the life of the Christian. Luther quickly saw that it was his meditation on Romans that had opened his eyes to the true nature of God's righteousness and the justification of the believer. The teachings of the Church had clouded these truths and so must be downgraded. It was Scripture that taught all things necessary for salvation and it was Scripture that should be recognized as the primary authority in the life of the Christian.

This, in turn, meant that Scripture should be accessible to the Christian and therefore should be translated into the vernacular tongue of the people. Up to now it had only been available in Latin and had only been encountered by ordinary people within the liturgy of the Mass. Luther saw the importance of translating the Bible into the German tongue and, through the printing press, making copies widely available to the German people. So when he was imprisoned in the Wartburg castle in 1521 he began the work of translation and produced what became the definitive version of the German Bible (the New Testament published in 1522 and the complete Bible in 1534). William Tyndale would shortly begin to do the same for the English people, producing the first English New Testament in 1525 (printed in Worms).

If the justified were known only to God it was therefore impossible for anyone else to know who was close to God and who was not. The doctrine of justification by faith had radical implications for the hierarchical structure of the medieval Church:

It is an invention that the Pope, bishop, priests and monks are called 'the spiritual estate', while princes, lords, craftsmen and farmers are called 'the secular estate'. This is a spurious idea, and nobody should fear it for the following reason. All Christians truly belong to the spiritual estate, and there is no difference among them apart from their office . . . We all have one baptism, gospel and faith which alone make us spiritual and a Christian people

> ... We are all consecrated priests through baptism ... Therefore someone who bears the status of a priest is nothing other than an officeholder. He takes priority for as long as he holds this office; when he is deposed, he becomes a peasant or citizen like all the others ... It follows from this that there is no basic difference between lay people, priests, princes and bishops, between the spiritual and the secular, except for their office and work and not on the basis of their status. (From *The Appeal to the German Nobility* (1520), in McGrath 1999, pp. 203–4)

This has become known as the doctrine of the priesthood of all believers and became a central feature of the new Reformation paradigm. With the abolition of the spiritual distinction between clergy and laity it became possible for clergy to marry and raise families. This Luther did, marrying a former nun, Katherine von Bora, in 1525.

But all of this did not mean that Luther became a radical egalitarian (as the Anabaptists were becoming). The invisibility of justification, and with it the invisibility of the true spiritual Church, led him to articulate the doctrine of the two kingdoms, one spiritual and one secular. On matters of salvation the spiritual kingdom held sway, but on earthly matters of day-to-day living the earthly kingdom, and especially the secular government of magistrates, princes and kings, held sway. Each were assigned to their own domain and were allowed jurisdiction within that domain. God wills both to exist side by side:

> For Luther, secular government includes much more than political authorities and governments; it includes everything that contributes to the preservation of this earthly life, especially marriage and family, the entire household, as well as property, business, and all the stations and vocations which God has instituted. Luther distinguishes all this from the spiritual reality of grace, of the word of God, and of faith and describes it as an 'external matter,' that is, related to our bodies, and also as the 'secular sword.'
>
> This secular or temporal government is necessary alongside the kingdom of Christ. 'For without it this life could not endure.' (Althaus 1972, p. 47)

When, therefore, the peasants rose up in revolt against their lords and appealed to Luther for support (1524), he was quick and harsh in his response: the princes were to use violent and coercive means to re-establish social order.

It is not possible in this book to tell the subsequent story of the spread of these ideas through the work of other reformers such as Huldrych Zwingli (1484–1532) in Zurich, Martin Bucer (1491–1551) in Strasbourg and England, and John Calvin (1509–64) in Geneva. (For an excellent account of the history of this whole period see MacCulloch 2003.) Two examples of the centrality of Luther's theology can simply be given. The first is Calvin stating that the doctrine of justification is 'the main hinge on which our religion turns' (Migliore 2005, p. 237). And the second is the appearance of the doctrine in a central position in the 39 Articles with *The Book of Common Prayer*:

> We are accounted righteous before God, only for the merit of our Lord and Saviour Jesus Christ by Faith, and not for our own works or deservings: Wherefore, that we are justified by Faith only is a most wholesome Doctrine, and very full of comfort, as more largely is expressed in the Homily of Justification. (Article XI)

Mission within the Protestant Reformation paradigm

Martin Luther believed that the only way to be saved and made a member of the Church is by the inward act of faith, a faith that does not belong to the realm of appearances. The true believer can never be distinguished with certainty from the hypocrite. This led Luther to develop the idea of the true Church being essentially an invisible body. He writes of the Church as 'a spiritual unity' which is 'not a physical assembly but an assembly of hearts in one faith'. There are two quite different ways, he says, of using the terms 'Church' and 'Christendom'. They can refer to the divinely instituted 'spiritual, internal Christendom' or to the man-made 'physical, external Christendom'. So Luther contrasted 'an assembly in a house, or in a parish, a bishopric, an archbishopric or a papacy' on the one hand, with 'the faith which makes true priests and Christians in the soul' on the other. (*On the Papacy in Rome*, from O'Donovan 1986, p. 89). The second, the essential Church, is a body whose actual membership is known only to God (see Figure 6).

Richard Field, Dean of Windsor and then Gloucester, who spanned the end

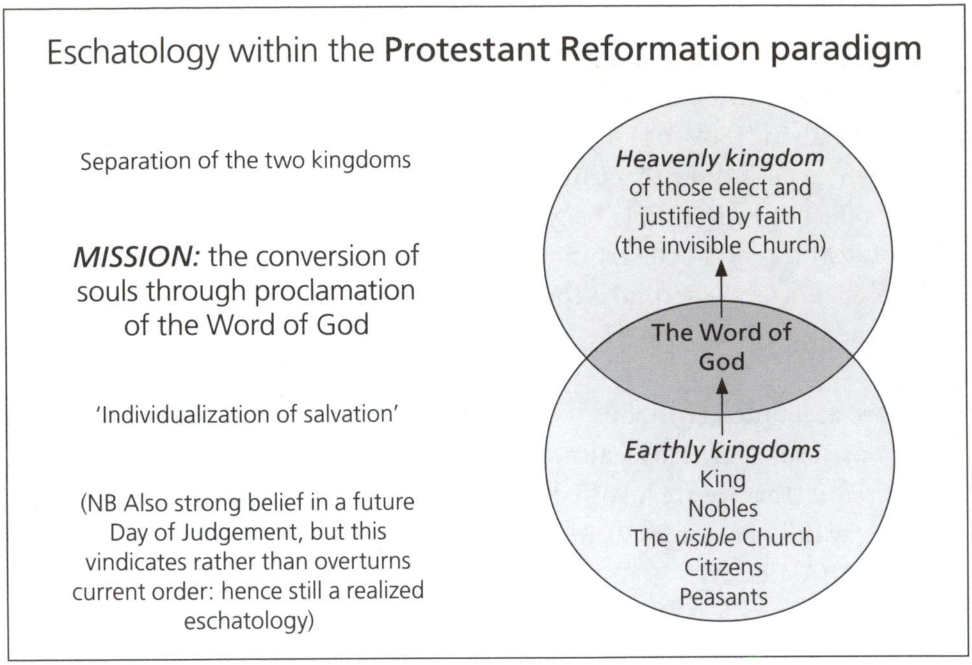

Eschatology within the **Protestant Reformation paradigm**

Separation of the two kingdoms

MISSION: the conversion of souls through proclamation of the Word of God

'Individualization of salvation'

(NB Also strong belief in a future Day of Judgement, but this vindicates rather than overturns current order: hence still a realized eschatology)

Heavenly kingdom
of those elect and justified by faith
(the invisible Church)

The Word of God

Earthly kingdoms
King
Nobles
The *visible* Church
Citizens
Peasants

Figure 6

of Elizabeth I's reign and the beginning of James I's, gave classical expression to this doctrine from an Anglican perspective:

> Hence it cometh that we say there is a visible and invisible Church, not meaning to make two distinct Churches, as our adversaries falsely and maliciously charge us, though the form of words may serve to insinuate some such thing, but to distinguish the divers considerations of the same Church; which, though it be visible in respect of the *profession* of supernatural verities revealed in Christ, use of holy Sacraments, order of Ministry, and due obedience yielded thereunto, and they discernible that do communicate therein; yet in respect of those most precious effects, and happy benefits of saving grace, wherein only the elect do communicate, it is invisible; and they that in so happy, gracious and desirable things have communion among themselves are not discernible from others to whom this fellowship is denied, but are known only to God. That Nathaniel was an Israelite all men knew; that he was *a true Israelite, in whom was no guile*, Christ only knew. (From More and Cross 1935, p. 41)

What of the mission of the visible Church? It was still desirable that it possess an outward and visible organization, membership of which should correspond as closely as possible to the true invisible Church, though identity was impossible. In the view of some of the Reformers the visible organization of the Church should as far as possible be of one type throughout Christendom, or at least throughout Reformed Christendom. In each nation or area of civil government this visible unity was to be secured by an 'established religion', determined by decree of the ruler, and on this basis the national churches on the Lutheran and Calvinist model were organized. Thomas Cranmer's writings provide a good example of this: he wrote of 'the Holy Church . . . unknown to the world', and also of 'the open known church' which is a 'register or treasury to keep the books of God's Holy Will and Testament' (from 'On the Lord's Supper', in O'Donovan 1986, p. 90; although O'Donovan points out that in Article 19 of the 39 Articles, he omitted to mention the invisible Church).

How was this visible Church to fulfil this role? In 1539 Luther wrote the following:

> Now, anywhere you hear or see [the Word of God] preached, believed, confessed, and acted upon, do not doubt that the true *ecclesia sancta catholica*, a 'holy Christian people' must be there, even though there are very few of them. For God's word 'shall not return empty' (Isaiah 55.11), but must possess at least a fourth or part of that field. And even if there were no other sign than this alone, it would be enough to prove that a holy Christian people must exist there, for God's word cannot be without God's people, and conversely, God's people cannot be without God's word. For who would preach the word, or hear it preached, if there were no people of God? And what could or would God's people believe, if there were no word of God? (*On the Councils and the Church*, in McGrath 1999, pp. 202–3)

This clearly shows the centrality of preaching to the life and mission of the Church. It is through preaching, both its delivery and its reception, that the visible Church approximates most closely to the true invisible Church and fulfils its vocation of being a herald of the latter. But this happens through God's action rather than the will of the preacher or congregation:

> The starting point of the Reformers' theology was not what people could or should do for the salvation of the world, but what God has already done in

> Christ. He visits the peoples of the earth with his light; he furthers his word so that it may 'run' and 'increase' till the last day dawns. The church was created by the *verbum externum* (God's word from outside humanity) and to the church this word has been entrusted. One might even say that it is the gospel itself which 'missionizes' and in this process enlists human beings . . . In this respect scholars often quote Luther's metaphor of the gospel being like a stone thrown into the water – it produces a series of circular waves which move out from the centre until they reach the furthest shore. In similar way the proclaimed word of God moves out to the ends of the earth . . . Throughout, then, the emphasis is on mission not being dependent on human efforts. (Bosch 1991, pp. 244–5)

Nevertheless, Christians are under an obligation to preach and teach the gospel 'to the erring pagans and non-Christians because of the duty of brotherly love' (ibid., p. 245).

It is important to note one more point in this mission type: there was to be a complete break with the idea of using force to Christianize people: the emperor's sword, Luther said, had nothing to do with faith and no army may attack others under the banner of Christ (though, as we have seen, coercion has its place in matters of secular power) (ibid., p. 245).

In the seventeenth century this approach to mission was developed in a significant way by the Moravians: this was a movement within German Protestantism which emphasized the practice of piety rooted in inner experience and expressing itself in a life of religious commitment. At Herrnhut, where they lived as a close-knit community, there were circles for devotional prayer, devotional Bible reading and a belief in the universal priesthood of all the faithful. There was also an anti-establishment ethos, seeking to move the Church away from a Christendom mentality. This was all an expression and development of the way the Reformation emphasized the importance of the individual's relationship with God (described by Küng as the individualization of salvation), but with a greater emphasis on the feelings/emotions of the heart than in the original reformers. A good example is Paul Gerhardt (1607–76), whose translation of a Latin poem became the famous hymn 'O Sacred Head, sore wounded'. The final verse provides a good illustration of the increasing individualization of salvation within the Protestant tradition:

In thy most bitter passion
My heart to thee doth cry,
With thee for my salvation
Upon the cross to die.
Ah, keep my heart thus movèd
To stand thy cross beneath,
To mourn thee, well-belovèd,
Yet thank thee for thy death.

Case study: the awakening of John Wesley

John Wesley (1703–91) provides a powerful example of many of these aspects of Protestant Reformation mission. While he was influenced by Enlightenment thinking and Catholic traditions at different points of his career, the heart of his theology and ministry shows him working within the Reformation tradition.

This is seen in the circumstances of his famous conversion or awakening at Aldersgate Street in London on 24 May 1736. He had been educated at Oxford where with other members of a 'Holy Club' he had developed a highly disciplined but dry devotional life. He had travelled to Georgia in the American Colonies as a missionary but had failed in that enterprise and returned home. In London he then had a profound inner experience which changed everything. In his journal he provides the following account:

> In the evening I went very unwillingly to a society in Aldersgate Street where one was reading Luther's *Preface to the Epistle to the Romans*. About a quarter before nine, while he was describing the change which God works in the heart through faith in Christ, I felt my heart strangely warmed, I felt I did trust in Christ, Christ alone for my salvation, and an assurance was given me that he had taken away *my* sins, even mine and saved *me* from the law of sin and death. I began to pray with all my might for those who had in a more especial manner despitefully used me and persecuted me. I then testified openly to all these what I now first felt in my heart. (In Turner 2002, pp. 27–8)

This famous passage is now regarded as one of the classical descriptions of an evangelical conversion experience, and it presents a vivid description of the heart of mission in the Protestant Reformation tradition. It shows how the receiving of the word of God was not meant just to inform the mind but was meant to bring about an inner awakening which converts the soul of the believer to a lifetime of devotion to Christ. Such an awakening is based on a deep awareness of the sinfulness and inadequacy of the believer, and it results in an awareness of one's own (rather than anyone else's) salvation.

The passage also demonstrates the ancestry of this tradition, for it was Luther who was being read at Aldersgate Street, and it was Luther writing on Paul's letter to the Romans.

A few days later Wesley was preaching at the University Church in Oxford (11 June 1738), and his sermon provides a clear insight into the kind of theology Wesley now espoused. It was later placed as the first of his 44 Sermons to be studied by local preachers, so is a very significant text. Revealingly, the sermon is entitled 'Salvation by Faith'. It begins with a series of assertions that recall Luther's train of thought in his monk's cell. Wesley draws a sharp contrast between the corruption of humankind and a man's efforts to atone for his sins – 'having nothing, neither righteousness nor works, to plead, his mouth is utterly stopped before God' – and the grace of God: 'All the blessings which God hath bestowed upon man are of His mere grace, bounty, or favour; His free, undeserved favour; favour altogether undeserved; man having no claim to the least of his mercies' (paragraphs 1–2).

He then provides a clear assertion of the doctrine of justification by grace through faith: '"By grace" then "are ye saved through faith." Grace is the source, faith the condition, of salvation' (paragraph 3).

A closeness to the Moravians (whom Wesley visited at Herrnhut in 1738) is seen in the way Wesley defines the nature of this faith. It is not simple assent to the existence of God and his judgement, nor assent to the divinity of Christ, nor to just living out the instructions of Christ:

> it is not barely a speculative, rational thing, a cold, lifeless assent, a train of ideas in the head; but also a disposition of the heart . . . a full reliance on the blood of Christ; a trust in the merits of His life, death, and resurrection; a recumbency upon Him as our atonement and our life, *as given for us*, and *living in us*; and, in consequence hereof, a closing with Him, and cleaving to Him, as our 'wisdom, righteousness, sanctification, and redemption,' or, in one word, our salvation. (*Sermons*, I.5)

It was this kind of vital faith that Wesley was now committed to living out. Henceforth his professed objective was 'to promote as far as I am able vital practical religion and by the grace of God to beget, preserve, and increase the life of God in the souls of men'. He did this through preaching, in churches, and then from 1739 in fields, in halls, up and down the country, covering some 250,000 miles on horseback (or in a carriage) over the course of his life. Here, again, in his concentration on preaching and the word we see continuity with the Reformation, though unlike the Reformers Wesley did not assume everyone in Europe had already heard the gospel. He was influenced by Jacobus Arminius, Dutch Reformed theologian, 1560–1609, who was a universalist rather than predestinarian Calvinist: every man and woman on the planet must be given the opportunity to be justified and sanctified by faith in Christ, not just those who think of themselves as the elect. He disregarded the parochial boundaries of the Church of England, ranging widely and freely up and down the country, famously declaring that 'I look upon all the world as my parish' (*Journal*, 3 July 1759).

Wesley also combined the doctrine of justification by faith with an emphasis on the pursuit of holiness to the point of Christian perfection: 'He that is, by faith, born of God *sinneth not*' (*Sermons*, II.6, italics mine). This doctrine of Christian perfectionism is distinctive to Wesley and provides an example of the way he developed the tradition he inherited.

Wesley's reliance on Scripture above reason and the tradition of the Church shows his continuity with the Reformation. While reason was also important to him it was kept firmly in its place below Scripture. Similarly in politics he was no radical child of the Enlightenment but remained a High Church Tory in politics. Nevertheless he achieved a remarkable rapport with the rural and industrial poor in his preaching. He was able to establish a system of 'class meetings' for the teaching and support of his followers, some 60 per cent of whom were women. He also commissioned a large number of itinerant preachers to extend his preaching. There were 114 of these by 1791, and the Methodist societies, as they came to be called, could number 72,000 members by 1791 (and 43,000 in America). His aim was to create a 'ginger group' that would renew the Church of England. It was only after his death that a formal separation took place between his Methodists, and the established Church. It is important to note that Wesley retained a huge respect for the role of the Sacraments of the Church of England in the life of the Methodist, and this was a key reason why he did not want them to split.

John's brother Charles Wesley (1707–88), the author of some 6,000 hymns and a key influence in the rise of Methodism, gave this whole approach to mission its most famous description in his great hymn 'And can it be'. This was written only hours after his own awakening to vital religion, on 21 May 1738 (three days before his brother). Drawing on the story of Peter being released from prison in Acts, the hymn is a prayer addressed to God and in praise of the atoning death of Christ on the cross. In a verse dropped from later reprints of the hymn (the second verse below), it shows the importance of personal feelings within evangelical conversion:

Long my imprisoned spirit lay
Fast bound in sin and nature's night;
Thine eye diffused a quickening ray, –
I woke, the dungeon flamed with light;
My chains fell off, my heart was free,
I rose, went forth, and followed Thee.

Still the small inward voice I hear,
That whispers all my sins forgiven;
Still the atoning Blood is near,
That quenched the wrath of hostile heaven.
I feel the life His wounds impart;
I feel my Saviour in my heart.

(Bradley 1990, pp. 37–9)

Some recent expressions of the type

The Protestant Reformation type of mission, as expressed and developed by John Wesley's approach to mission, has had a massive and increasing impact in the twentieth century. As we have seen, it is expressed through the preaching of the word, emphasizes an inner conversion manifested in changed feelings, and sits lightly to the structures of the established Church. The Pentecostal movement, as David Martin has recently argued (2002), is an extension of this type of church life, because it shares the emphasis on Scripture, on the doctrine of justification by faith (see Hollenweger 1972, ch. 23), and on the experiential dimension, magnifying this into a concern with a whole range of physical manifestations of faith. It also has minimal concern with the structures of the established churches.

In his classic study of Pentecostalism Walter Hollenweger presented the following vivid account of a typical experience of the Spirit within the movement. In many ways it describes the heart of what Pentecostalist mission seeks to nurture:

On 28 January, at about half past eleven at night, Jesus fulfilled his promise and baptized me with the Holy Spirit. This was the greatest experience of my life . . ., when I suddenly felt my shoulder shaking, and there was immediately a feeling like an electric shock from outside which went through my whole body and my whole being. I understood that the holy God had drawn near to me. I felt every limb of the lower half of my body shaking, and I felt involuntary movements and extraordinary power streaming through me. Through this power the shaking of my body grew continually, and at the same time the devotion of my prayer increased, to an extent that I had never experienced . . . My words dissolved in my mouth, and the quiet utterances of my prayer grew louder and changed into a foreign language. I grew dizzy. My hands, which I had folded in prayer, struck against the edge of the bed. I was no longer myself, although I was conscious the whole time of what was happening. My tongue jerked so violently that I believed it would be torn out of my mouth, yet I could not open my mouth of my own power. But suddenly I felt it opening, and words streamed out of it in strange languages. At first they came and went, with times of silence, but soon my voice grew louder and the words came quite clearly; they came like a stream from my lips. The voice grew louder and louder, at first sounding clear and bold, but suddenly changing into a terrible cry of distress, and I noticed that I was weeping. I was like a horn that someone was blowing . . . When it ceased it became quite silent, and there followed an almost silent prayer, which was also uttered in a strange language . . . When it was over my soul was filled with an inexpressible feeling of happiness and blessedness. I could do nothing but give thanks, give thanks aloud. The feeling of the presence of God was so wonderful, as if heaven had come down to earth. And indeed heaven was in my soul. (Hollenweger 1972, pp. 332–3)

This experience has been repeated with increasing frequency over the last fifty years in many parts of the world. Martin describes Pentecostalism and its associated expressions in charismatic Christianity as 'the largest global shift in the religious market over the last 40 years' (Martin 2002, p. xvii). It is estimated that Pentecostal numbers worldwide are increasing by around 19 million a year. On a conservative estimate it now encompasses a quarter of a billion people, mostly concentrated in the developing world. It is a fusion of the religion of poor whites with poor blacks that has become capable of crossing cultural barriers and becoming a global player, the most widespread form of Christianity after Roman Catholicism. Broadly speaking, according to Martin, Pentecostalism includes one in eight of the Christian 'constituency' of nearly two billion, and one in 25 of the global population as a whole. It is identified with a conservative understanding of Scripture and Christian living (see Jenkins 2002, but see also Yates 2005), but the heart of its distinctive appeal is an empowerment of the believer through spiritual gifts which are offered to all. It represent 'a fissiparous and peaceable extension of voluntarism and competitive pluralism' within the poor traditional societies where it is growing most strongly (Martin 2002, p. 1). Part of its strength comes from the way it fosters popular organization among the poorest members of society: 'Based on his study of new churches in Belém, Brazil, Andrew Chesnut argues that "in late twentieth-century Brazil, Pente-costalism stands out as one of the principal organizations of the poor". The churches provide a social network that would otherwise be lacking, and help teach members the skills they need to survive in a rapidly developing society' (Jenkins 2002, p. 44, quoting R. Andrew Chesnut, *Born Again in Brazil*, 1997).

It spreads partly inside the older churches and partly by 'breaking bounds' in every sense. It can be found within North America and Britain as well as the developing world. Within the established churches it is often called the char-ismatic movement and has recently found renewal through the Alpha Course, with its 'Holy Spirit weekend', vigorously and continuously promoted by Holy Trinity Church in Brompton, London.

As with Wesley, Scripture is central to Pentecostalism. Martin provides the following suggestive description of its use of Scripture:

People link their own stories and their group experiences to a narrative mov-ing from slavery to liberty, exile to restoration, and also from the dark domin-ion of the powers through the engagements of spiritual warfare to the empowerments of the kingdom. The kind of reverential and close reading of the Bible found among Pentecostals makes them familiar with its landscape, intimate friends with its characters regarded as people like themselves, and able to find all kinds of resources in its dreams, healings, and deliverances, its rebirths, prophecies, and expectations of future transformation. (Martin 2002, p. 6)

Martin then comments that in almost all these ways Pentecostalism is 'an extension' of Methodism and of the Evangelical Revivals (or Awakenings) of the eighteenth and early nineteenth centuries. 'In almost every respect Pentecostalism replicated Methodism: in its entrepreneurship and adaptability, lay participation and enthusiasm, and in its splintering and fractiousness. It did so in the place it offered to blacks and women and that in spite of the splintering over colour which occurred in both movements . . .' (ibid., pp. 8–9). Martin points out that Pentecostalism went beyond Methodism in its embracing of 'third blessing' baptism of the Holy Spirit, and of millennial expectation. 'Yet such differences may not be all that great. So far as millennial expectation is concerned, we find it present in early Methodism, and one cannot be sure how prominent it remains in contemporary Pentecostalism' (ibid., p. 9).

Summary of the Protestant Reformation paradigm

Context
Renaissance humanism, RC corruption, rise of commerce and the printing press.

Hierarchy of authorities
1. Scripture
2. Conscience/reason
3. Tradition

Methodology for theology
Exegesis of Scripture.

Eschatology
The salvation of the soul comes at the end for those individually justified by faith, but real assurance of this is given in the present.

Christology
Redemptive: Jesus the Lamb of God whose sacrificial death opens the way to salvation out of this world.

Discipleship
Justification by grace through faith in the cross of Christ and sanctification of the soul through a life of good works.

Mission of the Church
To be a herald of this salvation, especially through proclaiming the word: to be a signpost pointing to the invisible kingdom.

Ministry
Preaching of the word for individual conversion and ministry of the sacraments as signs of salvation.

Some examples
Luther, Wesley, Pentecostalism.

Debate

Galilean principles of the *missio Christi* (from p. 33)

1. Contemplative listening, which frames all ministry: listening to God, to other people, to oneself, especially in times of prayer and retreat.

2. Addressing society as a whole, at points where people live and work, including and especially the marginalized. This results in being received and accepted by some but rejected and opposed by others.

3. Pointing to the inaugurated yet still awaited kingdom, in word and in surprising saving deed (symbolic actions) which address the actual needs of people (both individual and structural); but without publicizing the wonders.

4. Calling for a personal response by all to the coming of this kingdom.

5. Doing all this through a collaborative team, who themselves are powerless and vulnerable and must suffer the consequences.

One response

1. Could it be claimed that Protestant Reformation mission is framed by listening, the listening to God, listening to others and listening to oneself described in the first Galilean principle? At crucial points it has been clear that real listening has taken place: Luther in his cell wrestling with the meaning of the word 'righteousness' in Romans 1.17, and then following through the implications of what he discovered; Wesley, back in London after the failure of his missionary work in Georgia, listening to the promptings of his heart in Aldersgate Street and then following through the theological implications of those promptings in his university sermon in Oxford; poor black and poor white Christians listening to the outpourings of the Holy Spirit in their Pentecostal worship and being empowered by these to create their own church communities. So, from the examples we have examined, it seems clear that the Protestant Reformation paradigm was born and was advanced by people paying attention to what God was doing among them and acting accordingly. And insofar as this tradition has remained true to the principle of the individual conscience being given a higher authority than the traditions of the Church, it could be argued that it has been very open to what 'the other' is saying in the secret places of the heart.

On the other hand, however, it could be argued that this mission type has emphasized proclamation more than listening to the other. Typically its missionaries have been convinced of the authority of their own understanding of the gospel and have sought to carry all before them. As an experiential movement it has not always seen the need to enter into dialogue with those it is seeking to win. The important point has been to facilitate a conversion experience within the hearts of potential converts, rather than an open-ended exploration of the faith. This must qualify the above to some extent.

2. Has society been addressed as a whole, at points where people live and work, including and especially the marginalized? A mixed answer can be given to this question: the early reformers removed the institution of the Church from a direct involvement in the relationship between the believer and God, and so allowed anyone and everyone to have access to divine grace. In this sense they were universalists. But they did not encourage missionary work within their own territories. There was an assumption that the population was already Christian and, as magisterial Protestants, they believed this population had a

duty to obey the ruler. Those movements within the Reformation which sought to win over the hearts and minds of the population against the king or prince, such as the Anabaptists, were generally crushed. While in principle, then, early Protestantism was meant to be offered to everyone, in practice this was not the case. It was left to later Protestants, such as those caught up in the revivals, and especially Whitfield and Wesley and their followers, to take the gospel to where people lived and worked, including (and in Wesley's case especially) the marginalized. This they did, with remarkable success. In the twentieth century it can be argued that Pentecostalism has extended this mission around the globe, to the extent that it is now the fastest growing branch of Christianity.

3. Does the Protestant Reformation mission type point to the inaugurated yet still awaited kingdom, in word and in surprising saving deed (symbolic actions), addressing the actual needs of people? Again, a mixed answer can be given: Luther was very clear in his separation of the heavenly kingdom and the visible Church: the latter belonged to the earthly kingdom and could only point to the invisible church of true believers which belonged to the heavenly kingdom. The mission of the visible Church was to be a herald of the latter, pointing to it in its preaching and sacraments. On this point, then, he scored highly. But the Lutheran Reformation lacked signs and wonders, such as healings or deliverances, to supplement the preaching. Miraculous happenings were few and far between and, when they occurred, were more often than not associated with witchcraft. Again it was in later centuries that there was a recovery of the physical dimension of heralding the kingdom. The pietism of the Moravians and Wesley's recognition of the centrality of feeling to faith paved the way, but it was not until the rise of the charismatic and Pentecostal movements in the twentieth century that the physical healings and signs found in the Gospels were again experienced within the Church. But Pentecostalism has more than made up for this neglect in the past: 'To attend a Pentecostal service, where the Spirit descends upon and among the congregation, is to hear and see the unloosing of authentic forces that seem to emerge from the recesses of being' (Harold Bloom, quoted in Martin 2002, p. 9).

However, it can be asked if genuine healing takes place. Does this type of mission really change people's lives for the better, or does it just soothe the pain? Some have argued that it does not address people's real needs because it does not seek to change the conditions and the structures within which they live. It may make them feel better for a day, but the underlying causes of their sicknesses and oppressions remain. Wesley, for example, has been accused of defusing a much needed political and social revolution in England (e.g. Thompson 1968). He was, as we have noted, a Tory all his life and upheld the hierarchy of the day. Similarly Pentecostalism in Latin America has been accused of defusing the radicalism of the liberation theology movement. On the other hand Methodism was one of the principal sources of the Labour Movement in Britain, which bore rich fruit for the poor in the twentieth century. And we have already seen Andrew Chesnut argue that in Brazil Pentecostalist churches provide a social network that would otherwise be lacking.

However, does this type of mission, with its emphasis on the inner life of the soul, have the resources to address political needs and opportunities? The twenty-first century faces huge environmental needs and an increasing polarization of Islam and Christianity in many parts of the world. Can the Protestant Reformation tradition draw the Christian community into real engagement with these kinds of issues? There must be real questions here.

4. As far as the fourth Galilean principle is concerned, it has been clear from the start that this type of mission revolves around the making of a personal response by the believer to the proclamation of the kingdom. Luther and the other reformers renounced the use of coercion in mission and so opened the possibility of a free and genuine response. This has generally been maintained ever since (though some missionaries have sought to engineer the atmosphere within mass meetings). Compared to its predecessor this mission type scores highly on this point.

5. Finally, with its doctrine of the priesthood of all believers, taken up and propagated enthusiastically ever since, the Protestant Reformation paradigm laid the basis for a collaborative approach to ministry. In practice this has not always been the case, with Magisterial Protestantism retaining a strongly hierarchical approach to church government and ministry and, in the case of Anglicanism and certain parts of the Lutheran Church, a retention of the threefold hierarchical order of ministry found in Catholicism. However, in Methodism, and subsequently in the untidy and pluralistic world of Pentecostalism, there have been many opportunities for disadvantaged members of society to play a vital part in the mission and ministry of the Church.

Overall, then, this mission type has scored highly in comparison to the other types. This should not be surprising as the Protestant Reformation paradigm was, from the start, a deliberate attempt to recover the essential character of primitive Christianity. However, we have noted a question over the depth of its commitment to listening as well as speaking, and some serious questions over whether it has the resources to address political needs and opportunities of the twenty-first-century world.

Discussion questions

Are there local contexts today where this type of mission may nevertheless be just what is needed?
What might the strengths and weaknesses of this type of mission be within your own local context?

Further reading

Althaus, Paul (1972), *The Ethics of Martin Luther*, Fortress

Anderson, Allan (2004), *An Introduction to Pentecostalism: Global Charismatic Christianity*, Cambridge University Press

Avis, Paul (2000), *The Anglican Understanding of the Church*, SPCK

Bevans, Stephen B., and Roger P. Schroeder (2004), *Constants in Context: A Theology of Mission for Today*, Orbis

Book of Common Prayer (1662), standard edition, Cambridge University Press

Bosch, David J. (1991), *Transforming Mission: Paradigm Shifts in Theology of Mission*, Orbis

Bradley, Ian (1990), *The Penguin Book of Hymns*, Penguin

Hill, Jonathan (2003), *The History of Christian Thought*, Lion

Hollenweger, Walter J. (1972), *The Pentecostals*, SCM Press

Jenkins, Philip (2002), *The Next Christendom: The Coming of Global Christianity*, Oxford University Press

Jenkins, Simon (2000), *England's Thousand Best Churches*, Penguin

Kelly, J. N. D. (1977), *Early Christian Doctrines*, 5th edn, A & C Black

Küng, Hans (1995), *Christianity: Its Essence and History*, SCM Press

MacCulloch, Diarmaid (2003), *Reformation: Europe's House Divided 1490–1700*, Allen Lane

McGrath, Alistair (1999), *Reformation Thought: An Introduction*, 3rd edn, Blackwell

Martin, David (2002), *Pentecostalism: The World Their Parish*, Blackwell

Migliore, Daniel (2005), *Faith Seeking Understanding: An Introduction to Christian Theology*, 2nd edn, Eerdmans

Miles, Margaret (2005), *The Word Made Flesh: A History of Christian Thought*, Blackwell

More, Paul Elmer, and Frank Leslie Cross, eds (1935), *Anglicanism*, SPCK

O'Donovan, Oliver (1986), *On the Thirty Nine Articles*, Paternoster

Stott, John (1986), *Christian Mission in the Modern World*, Kingsway

Thomas, Norman, ed. (1995), *Readings in World Mission*, SPCK

Thompson, E. P. (1968), *The Making of the English Working Class*, Penguin

Tomlin, Graham (2002), *Luther and His World*, Lion

Turner, John Munsey (2002), *John Wesley: The Evangelical Revival and the Rise of Methodism in England*, Epworth

Wesley, John (1944), *Sermons on Several Occasions (44 Sermons)*, Epworth

Yates, Timothy, ed. (2005), *Mission and the Next Christendom*, Cliff College

9

Building the Kingdom on Earth Enlightenment Modern Mission

In September 1942 William Temple, the Archbishop of Canterbury, rose to address a packed Royal Albert Hall under the banner 'The Church Looks Forward'. He was joined on the platform by Sir Stafford Cripps, a member of the war-time government and a future Chancellor of the Exchequer in the post-war Labour government. Temple had recently published a Penguin special, *Christianity and Social Order*, which was selling in its tens of thousands and was making an impact on general thinking about the kind of society to be established in Britain after the end of the war. Temple's own proposals, described in the book and reiterated on the platform of the Albert Hall, had been seen and approved by John Maynard Keynes, the dominant economist of the era, and William Beveridge, the academic and civil servant whose Beveridge Report put in place the key ideas behind the creation of the welfare state. Temple himself had been the one to coin the phrase 'the welfare state' in lectures of 1928. Through all of this he showed that he not only spoke on behalf of the churches but represented a wider movement in British society that was not prepared to tolerate a return to the pre-war society, where huge inequalities had resulted in desperate poverty and squalor in many British cities. Instead he gave voice to a general aspiration that everyone in Britain should be decently housed, healthy, well educated and provided with financial security into their old age.

Temple's speech was received with great excitement and widely reported in the national press the following day. Some of his remarks about the need to restrict the way the banking sector could issue credit were criticized in the City of London. But this only served to draw more attention to his case and its impact increased as he repeated the speech to packed halls in Birmingham, Leicester and Edinburgh, between September 1942 and October 1943. Temple died in 1944, but after the war, with the election of the Labour Government, the programme of social reform that he advocated began to be implemented, not least through the founding of the National Health Service. Temple is credited with being one of the architects of the welfare state.

This scene from the Albert Hall in 1942 is a picture of a distinctive mission type, the next to be examined in this book. It is an approach to mission concerned as much about the physical and mental conditions in which people live as their spiritual lives. It is rooted in what Küng calls the Enlightenment Modern Christian paradigm, itself formed by key ideas of the eighteenth-century Enlightenment in European culture. It was a hugely influential approach to mission in the nineteenth and early twentieth centuries, leading to the construction of schools, hospitals and other educational and medical work all around the world and also propelling Christian laity and clergy into the forefront of social reform in the West. With Temple's contribution to the founding of the welfare state in Britain this mission type arguably reached the height of its influence. This chapter will trace its roots in the Enlightenment and give examples of its expression within the churches through the whole period. It will look especially at Temple's role and at the theology behind his social action. It will also give more recent examples of the type, showing how it has continued to be influential and has formed many in today's churches.

Background

The Enlightenment in European culture: a sketch

In some ways the Protestant Reformation provided the seedbed of the Enlightenment modern paradigm. This was through its theology of the two kingdoms and the way this brought about an increasing separation of civil and spiritual realms. The Church was to be concerned with the latter, while the state and civil society were concerned with the former. On political, economic, social and even moral questions the Church was gradually sidelined: its concern was to be with the things of heaven rather than the earth.

This resulted in the Catholic Church losing control of scientific endeavour. The Reformation and post-Reformation era in Europe saw the blossoming of scientific exploration across the continent, with early pioneers like Leonardo da Vinci (1452–1519), Copernicus (1473–1543), Galileo (1564–1642) and Kepler (1571–1630) opening up new fields for exploration. Copernicus is especially representative of this movement because, as mentioned at the start of this book, his cosmology removed the earth from the centre of the universe. Humanity found itself to be living on a moving and rather more mysterious planet from the one it had grown up in. The only security now lay in the power of human reason to try and solve some of its mysteries. This Copernican revolution in Western thought simultaneously removed humanity from the centre of a hierarchical universe and made humanity's power of reason the measure of all things.

The work of Sir Isaac Newton (1642–1726) represents both the climax of this enquiry and its elevation to a whole new plane of understanding. He demonstrated the success of scientific reasoning in understanding and regulating the world around us, and the need for that reasoning to reach into all other aspects of human life. The Enlightenment as a wider philosophical and cultural movement was born out of this success.

Philosophical developments began with the *empiricism* of Francis Bacon (1561–1626), who argued that the only kind of knowledge that science can rely upon is gained through sensory observation. This led to the elimination of the notion of purpose from nature: explanations were to be in terms of mechanistic causes and effects rather than divine goals and intentions.

The *dualism* of René Descartes (1596–1650) was another philosophical development: he decided to rely solely on human reason and doubt everything else. This led him to formulate his famous maxim '*cogito, ergo sum*', 'I think therefore I am'. It is important to note the individualism of this statement: it is not the community's thinking that becomes the basis of knowledge but the reasoning of the individual mind. This led him to formulate a philosophy that became known as Cartesianism, in which a sharp distinction is drawn between the subject who looks out on the world, and the object that he or she looks at. In his philosophy the thinking, observing subject tries to make sense of the objective world 'out there'. This resulted in a basic separation between the human and non-human world.

Bosch provides a helpful summary of key features within this new way of thinking:

- it was, pre-eminently, the Age of *Reason*, where reason was seen as belonging not only to 'believers' but to all human beings;
- it operated with the *subject–object* scheme, in which nature ceased to be 'creation' and was no longer people's teacher, but became the object of their analysis;
- it eliminated *purpose* from science, introducing direct causality as the clue to understanding reality;
- it believed in the notion of *progress*, with exploration of the world as well as science opening up new possibilities for human living, convincing many that humanity had the ability and the will to remake the world in its own image;
- scientific knowledge was regarded as *factual, value-free and neutral*, and as really the only kind of knowledge that counts;
- *all problems were in principle solvable*, though it would take time to solve them;
- and human beings are now *emancipated, autonomous individuals*.

Taken together these ideas represent a revolution in European thought: the Age of Reason saw an increasing turn away from supernatural revelation as the source of truth, and an increasing suspicion of medieval thought as stifling. 'In Augustine and Luther the individual was . . . regarded, first and foremost, as standing in a relationship to God and the church. Now individuals became important and interesting to themselves' (Bosch 2002, pp. 264–7).

Immanuel Kant (1724–1804) provided the most sophisticated and powerful description of the scope of reason in his *Critique of Pure Reason* (1781). In this work he sought to map the limits of what reason can do, but paradoxically he also strengthened its scope and authority within those limits.

The Enlightenment also saw the rise of historical consciousness, developing out of the critical study of history, including the Bible. Thinkers became aware of the developing nature of human society, stretching back through many ages. If this age was different from and better than the preceding one, this showed that something called history existed and that it could be studied in a critical way. Edward Gibbon (1737–94) author of the great *The History of the Decline and Fall of the Roman Empire* (first part published in 1776) is the most famous example: he gave materialistic rather than spiritual explanations for the decline of Rome and the rise of Christianity.

There were huge political consequences as well. The rise of individualism implied the rise of democratic ideals and the overthrow of the medieval monarchies. In France the philosopher Rousseau began his treatise *The Social Contract* (1762) with the rallying call 'Man was born free but is everywhere in chains.' This way of thinking helped to precipitate a number of struggles for freedom from the shackles of kings and popes. The two most significant examples were the American War of Independence (1775–83) and the French Revolution (1789). This age saw the rise of the democratic ideal, in which the autonomous individual would control the government of the nation. Tom Paine's *The Rights of Man* (1791–2) became one of the most influential texts behind these political movements.

But another consequence of scientific breakthroughs was the rise of technology, for example in the great inventions that created Lancashire's cotton industry: Watt's steam engine, Kay's flying shuttle, Hargreave's spinning jenny, Cartwright's power loom (all between 1733 and 1785). These led to the rise of industrialization, resulting in major social changes as rural populations moved to the new factories in the cities, in England first and then in Germany.

Commercial expansion overseas followed in the nineteenth century, which carried Western culture, philosophy and education to many points around the globe. The Age of Reason became the Age of Empire, which harnessed technology and industrialization for the scramble for global domination by the European powers in the late nineteenth century.

Finally, it is necessary to mention an alternative side to the Enlightenment, a fascination with interior feelings and emotions. The seeds of this are seen in the introspection of St Ignatius Loyola (who founded the Jesuits in 1540), and in the *intuitionism* of Blaise Pascal (1623–62), who stated that 'the heart has its reasons that reason cannot know'. The individualism of the Enlightenment encouraged this turn inwards, and resulted in the eruption of Romanticism in art and literature in the late eighteenth and early nineteenth centuries: a movement reasserting passion and imagination in reaction to the rationalism of the Age of Reason. Romanticism is a mood or tendency rather than a system of thought and is found first in German literature, especially in Goethe. Its influence spread quickly to England and is seen in the work of Blake, Wordsworth, Coleridge, Shelley and Keats. In France the writings of Chateaubriand and Victor Hugo also provide examples.

Developments in Christian thinking: the example of Hegel

The Enlightenment's elevation of reason had a profound influence on Protestant thinking in eighteenth- and nineteenth-century Europe. It is possible to trace two fundamental responses: the first was 'to divorce religion from reason, locating it in *human feeling and experience*, and thus protect it from any possible attacks by the Enlightenment's tendency toward "objectifying consciousness"' (Bosch 1991, p. 269). This was the response of the Pietist movement and the evangelical awakenings, which had their roots in the Protestant Reformation paradigm but like the Romantics looked to interior feelings for the authenticating marks of faith (see above, p. 122). Friedrich Schleiermacher (1768–1834), the German Reformed theologian based in Berlin and often described as 'the father of modern theology', provided a brilliant and extended theological description of this response in his writings. He described true religion as 'the feeling of absolute dependence upon God' and interpreted and presented the theology of the Protestant Reformation tradition through this lens.

The other response, which helped to form the new Enlightenment modern Christian paradigm and its distinctive type of Christian mission, was to do the opposite and *marry* religion with reason, claiming that the most rational form of living was a religious one and specifically the Christian one. The best example of this response is found in the writings of one of Schleiermacher's contemporaries in Berlin, the Christian philosopher George Wilhelm Friedrich Hegel (1770–1831). He began his career at Jena (1801), where he wrote his pioneering masterpiece *The Phenomenology of Mind* (1806), then moved to Nuremberg, working as a headmaster of a high school (teaching his pupils philosophy among other subjects: what they made of this is not recorded). His reputation as a philosopher grew through this period and in 1816 he was appointed Professor of Philosophy at Heidelberg and then, in 1818, to a similar post in Berlin, becoming an awkward colleague of Schleiermacher. He remained in Berlin until his death, becoming the dominant philosopher of his generation. His writings include *Science of Logic* (1816), *The Philosophy of Right* (1819), a treatise on social and political matters, and the *Encyclopedia of the Philosophical Sciences* (between 1817 and 1830), a vast compendium of knowledge presented within the categories of his system.

Hegel believed that behind the whole of reality was a unifying and rational mind or spirit, which he called *geist* (which Peter Singer translates as 'mind': see Singer 1983). This led him to state that 'whatever is rational is real and whatever is real is rational'. He believed that all things *tend* to the complete and perfect design of this mind by a logical process.

Hegel goes beyond his contemporaries and is highly significant because he saw this process as working itself out through history: 'in contrast to Kant, who thought he could say on purely philosophical grounds what human nature is and always must be, Hegel accepted Schiller's suggestion that the very foundations of the human condition could change from one historical era to another. This notion of change, of development throughout history, is fundamental to Hegel's view of the world' (Singer 1983, p. 9). Friedrich Engels, looking back on Hegel's importance to himself and to his colleague Karl Marx, confirms this assessment:

> What distinguished Hegel's mode of thinking from that of all other philosophers was the exceptional historical sense underlying it. However abstract and idealist the form employed, the development of his ideas runs always parallel to the development of world history, and the latter is indeed supposed to be only the proof of the former. (Singer 1983, p. 9)

But *how* did he see all things tending to the complete and perfect design of mind/spirit through history? Hegel postulated the existence of a unifying process that he called the 'dialectic'. In this process an original tendency, or 'thesis', gives rise to its opposite tendency, an 'antithesis'. Both are then resolved into a higher unity, a 'synthesis'. This takes place through the unfolding process of world history. So, for example, he interpreted recent events, and especially the rise of Napoleon, as the synthesis of the old monarchies (the thesis), the French Revolution upturning the old order (the antithesis), and the rise of Napoleon as the synthesis of the two and a step forward for the life of Europe and especially for Prussia.

Hegel believed his era was one of great progress and promise, based on the increasing dominance of reason over human affairs:

> Never since the sun has stood in the firmament and the planets revolved around it had it been perceived that man's existence centres in his head, i.e. in

thought, inspired by which he builds up the world of reality . . . not until now had man advanced to the recognition of the principle that thought ought to govern spiritual reality. This was accordingly a glorious mental dawn. All thinking beings shared in the jubilation of this epoch. (*Lectures in the Philosophy of History*, in Singer 1983, p. 21)

Crucially, though, Hegel understood this unfolding dialectic to be taking place within a wider frame, the divine history of God's reconciliation of all creation. He understood this history to be taking place in three stages:

(1) First, in and for itself, God [is] in his eternity before the creation of the world and outside the world.

(2) Second, God creates the world and posits the separation. He creates both nature and finite spirit. What is thus created is at first an other, positive outside of God. But God is essentially the reconciling to himself of what is alien, what is particular, what is posited in separation from him. He must restore to freedom and to his truth what is alien, has fallen away in the idea's self-diremption [forcible separation] in its falling away from itself. This is the path and the process of reconciliation.

(3) In the third place, through this process of reconciliation, spirit has reconciled with itself what is distinguished from itself in its act of diremption, of primal division, and thus it is the Holy Spirit, the Spirit [present] in its community.

These are not external distinctions, which *we* have made merely in accord with what we are; rather, they are the activity, the developed vitality, of absolute spirit itself. (From Hegel's 1827 Lectures on the Philosophy of Religion, quoted in Hodgson 2005, p. 128)

Hegel, then, was not just a philosopher of the secular world, but articulated a theological philosophy, in which Christian doctrine was given a place. In the passage above, for example, a Trinitarian perspective plays a large part in forming the philosophical language and framework. Overall, Hegel provides one of the most sophisticated and comprehensive integrations of theology and philosophy and provides a deeply impressive foundation for the Enlightenment modern paradigm of Christian life and thought (see further Hodgson 2005).

He has also had a wide and recurring influence within both philosophy and theology as well as further afield. Peter Singer has written that

> No philosopher of the nineteenth or twentieth centuries has had as great an impact on the world as Hegel. The only possible exception to this sweeping statement would be Karl Marx – and Marx himself was heavily influenced by Hegel. Without Hegel, neither the intellectual nor the political developments of the last 150 years would have taken the path they did. (Singer 1983, p. vii)

Examples of this influence would be the nineteenth-century schools of German Idealism and British Idealism, which came to form the thinking of William Temple among many others. Within theology his dialectical approach to history has influenced twentieth-century movements, such as process theology (mediated through the philosophy of A. N. Whitehead). Contemporary theologians such as Jürgen Moltmann and Wolfhart Pannenberg show his influence, with their replacement of the Lutheran two-kingdoms theology with an understanding of the kingdom of God present within and realized through human history (e.g. Moltmann 1967; Pannenberg 1967).

Mission within the Enlightenment modern paradigm

The Enlightenment's belief in progress, and especially in European culture's progress within science, technology, philosophy and politics, had a major influence on the development of a new type of mission within the churches. Bosch describes this influence in the following way:

> Perhaps the optimism of the Enlightenment's philosophy of *progress* is the element more clearly recognisable in modern theology and the contemporary church than any of the elements listed so far. The idea of the imminent this-worldly global triumph of Christianity is a recent phenomenon and intimately related to the modern spirit. Sometimes it manifested itself as the belief that the entire world would soon be converted to the Christian faith [as in the World Missionary Conference at Edinburgh in 1910]; at other times Christianity was regarded as an irresistible power in the process of reforming

the world, eradicating poverty, and restoring justice for all. This latter program was pursued particularly where God was seen as a benevolent Creator, people as intrinsically capable of moral betterment, and the kingdom of God as the crown of the steady progression of Christianity. The spread of 'Christian *knowledge*' would suffice in achieving these aims. (Bosch 1991, p. 271)

Expressions of this type can be drawn from both the early and later parts of the era. From the early Enlightenment Bosch cites the philosopher Leibnitz (1646–1716) who described the Church's task in the world as *propagatio fidei per scientiam* (the propagation of Christianity through science or knowledge). A second example is Thomas Bray founding the Society for Promoting Christian Knowledge in 1698

to promote and encourage the erection of charity schools in all parts of England and Wales; to disperse, both at home and abroad, Bibles and tracts of religion; and in general to advance the honour of God and the good of mankind, by promoting Christian knowledge both at home and in the other parts of the world by the best methods that should offer. (Quoted in 'SPCK', *Oxford Dictionary of the Christian Church*, 3rd edn, 1997)

It is equating the advance of the honour of God and the good of mankind with the building of schools and the teaching of knowledge that is so revealing and distinctive and makes this quotation typical of its age.

This educational work was extended in 1807 by the founding of the British and Foreign Schools Society, a mainly Nonconformist body, and in 1811 by the founding of the National Society for the Education of the Poor in the Principles of the Established Church. These societies came to pioneer the provision of elementary education in England and Wales before there was any system of state education. The National Society also started to train teachers from 1841. In all of this it is the investment of the churches' time and resources, at local as well as national level, that is revealing and significant. The increasing provision of education became one of the most significant forms of mission by the churches in nineteenth-century Britain. As Bosch writes, 'Through knowledge and education benevolence and charity would be spread far and wide. God's kingdom became increasingly aligned with the culture and civilization of the West' (1991, p. 271).

Case study: William Temple and the founding of the welfare state

A good example of this approach to mission comes a century later in the figure of William Temple, whose own father, Frederick Temple (also an archbishop of Canterbury), came to prominence through his educational work. William's rootedness in the Enlightenment belief in progress, mediated through Hegelian Idealism and meshed with Christian doctrine, is demonstrated by the following heady quotation from an early point in his career:

> We may expect then that the course of history will continue in the future, as in the past, to consist in the conversion of nations, the building of the Christian state, and the incorporation of the Christian states within the fellowship of the Church, until at last Christendom and humanity are interchangeable terms. Then, as the Divine life of which the Church is the channel leavens all things, the Holy City will be realized, descending from God, the New Jerusalem which is the moral and social life of mankind made perfect in the love of God. (Temple 1917, p. 332)

The concept of Christendom, then, has returned, replacing the two-kingdoms theology of the Reformation. But unlike the medieval Catholic paradigm, which saw Christendom as a fixed and stable order that would last for ever, this outlook saw Christendom brought about by the progress and development of human civilization, reaching its consummation at a future point. The moral and social life of human societies was to make an intrinsic and necessary contribution to the kingdom, a contribution that would gradually reach around the globe and encompass more and more of the peoples of the earth. Mission, within this grand vision, was to be the developmental work of helping *to build the kingdom on earth* (see Figure 7).

This vision shows the influence of Temple's teachers at university. As an undergraduate at Balliol College, Oxford, he came under the influence of T. H. Green's philosophy. Green had been a philosophy tutor at the college in the 1870s and had also been involved in work for social reform in the poor districts of Oxford. He and those who followed him in the college believed that they were training young men to be public servants, in government, church and law. The

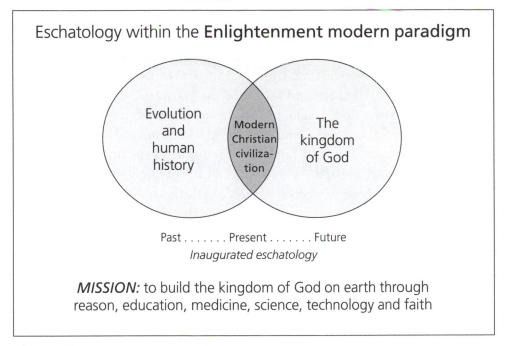

Figure 7

Idealist philosophy they learnt, based ultimately on Hegel, saw human society within a historical context: the nation was caught up in a process of purposive growth, and the role of public servants was to work for the increasing realization of the perfect society that was slowly emerging. When Temple arrived at Balliol the Scottish philosopher Edward Caird was head of the college and was continuing to teach this morally serious and empowering outlook. Temple became one of its leading representatives. A number of Temple's books incorporate this philosophy with theology, the most significant examples being *Mens Creatrix* (Creative Mind) of 1917, *Christus Veritas* (Christ the Truth) of 1924, and the Gifford Lectures, *Nature, Man and God*, of 1934.

Temple is significant because he not only provided a philosophical and theological articulation of this mission type, but in his ministry and political involvement put it into practice in an influential way. This was seen at the start of this chapter where his role in the founding of the welfare state was mentioned. A few more details on this work can make the point even clearer. It was expressed in a significant way when he was bishop of Manchester and chaired the large ecumenical conference of 1924 on politics, economics and citizenship (COPEC). With other church leaders he then intervened in the Coal Strike of 1926 to try and bring the different sides together, but this was not successful. When he was archbishop of York, from 1929, he looked for more opportunities to take this work forward and in 1941 called the Malvern Conference, on post-war social reconstruction. It had an impressive group of speakers, including T. S. Eliot, Dorothy L. Sayers, and Donald Mackinnon. The conference was poorly managed, and the final resolution was quite vague but, as John Kent writes, it had a wider impact: 'As far as the Church of England was concerned, Malvern undoubtedly expressed a resurgence of the more radical Anglican attitudes to unemployment and poverty which had dropped into the background after 1926' (Kent 1992, p. 161). Arising out of that conference he then wrote the Penguin Special *Christianity and Social Order*, which went on to sell 139,000 copies, and launched the 'Church Looks Forward' campaign. This campaign took place after Temple's translation to Canterbury and, as we saw, made a significant impact. He called for the provision of decent housing, family allowances, increased wages, milk and one good meal a day at school, education to the age of 18, unemployment provision, representation for workers on the directorates through the unions, and two days' rest in seven for every citizen. He was clearly determined that the opportunity of the moment should not be lost (as it had been lost after the First World War and after the strikes of 1926).

David Jenkins, who subsequently became bishop of Durham, wrote how, as a teenager, he attended the Albert Hall meeting, 'and what I drew from this, as well as what I read of his utterances and writings, was a clear understanding that we should be deeply Christian and deeply concerned with current affairs' (Jenkins 1981, pp. 321–2). Similarly Edward Heath wrote that 'The impact of William Temple on my generation was immense . . . The reason was not far to seek. William Temple was foremost among the leaders of the nation, temporal or spiritual, in posing challenging, radical questions about the nature of our society. Most important of all, he propounded with lucidity and vigour his understanding of the Christian ethic in its application to the contemporary problems which engrossed us all' (Temple 1976, Foreword).

Furthermore, as we also noted, within the space of five years many of the social and economic objectives advocated by Temple had been achieved. These included the creation of a national health service, the nationalization of principal industrial resources such as the coal industry, and major improvements in social security to cover every eventuality between the cradle and the grave (including child allowances). Taken as a whole these measures amounted to the creation of the welfare state, in which the evils of want, destitution and hunger were banished from post-war society. There were, of course, other powerful forces behind these developments, but William Temple and those who supported him showed that the Church was both a significant herald and an instrument of their coming about (see Spencer 2001, and Grimley 2004, pp. 225ff.).

Some recent expressions of the type

The second half of the twentieth century has also seen this type of mission promoted in various parts of the worldwide Church, though in very different ways. One influential example comes from the World Council of Churches in its 1967 report *The Church for Others*. This report suggested that God is at work in the historical process, that the purpose of his mission is the establishment of social harmony, this social harmony is identical with the kingdom of God, and that it is exemplified in 'the emancipation of coloured [*sic*] races, the concern for the humanisation of industrial relations, various attempts at rural development, the quest for business and professional ethics, the concern for intellectual honesty and integrity' (in Stott 1986, p. 17). Moreover, in working towards this goal God uses 'men and women both inside and outside the churches', and the Church's particular role in the mission of God is to 'point to God at work in world history', to discover what he is doing, to catch up with it and to get involved in it ourselves. For God's primary relationship is to the world, and 'it is the world that must be allowed to provide the agenda for the churches' (ibid.). In other words, the churches should seek to serve the world by joining with others in meeting contemporary social needs: the Church is not a master but a servant of others.

Liberation theology

Parts of the Roman Catholic world also embraced this kind of socially and historically rooted outlook. The initial impetus came from the Second Vatican Council of 1961–65 and especially its document *Gaudium et Spes*, which, in rousing language, called on the Church to turn outwards to the world in which it lived:

> The joys and hopes, the grief and anguish of the people of our time, especially of those who are poor or afflicted, are the joys and hopes, the grief and anguish of the followers of Christ as well. Nothing that is genuinely human fails to find an echo in their hearts . . . they cherish a feeling of deep solidarity with the human race and with its history. (*Vatican Council II* 1996, p. 163)

The bishops of Latin America responded to this call and turned with solidarity to the specific context of their own continent which, in the 1960s, was sharply divided between rich elites ruling through harsh military dictatorships and the majority poor who were now struggling for justice and liberation. As the bishops opened their vision and hearts to this polarized context they initiated the liberation theology movement. In their statement from their conference at Medellín in 1968 they stated that

> Latin America is obviously under the sign of transformation and development; a transformation that, besides taking place with extraordinary speed, has come to touch and influence every level of human activity, from the economic to the religious.
>
> This indicates that we are on the threshold of a new epoch in this history of Latin America. It appears to be a time of zeal for full emancipation, of liberation from every form of servitude, of personal maturity and of collective integration.

In ringing tones the bishops then described a divine presence within this historical movement:

> We cannot fail to see in this gigantic effort toward a rapid transformation and development an obvious sign of the Spirit who leads the history of humankind and of the peoples toward their vocation. We cannot but discover in this force, daily more insistent and impatient for transformation, vestiges of the image of God in human nature as a powerful incentive. This dynamism leads us progressively to an even greater control of nature, a more profound personalisation and fellowship, and an encounter with the God who ratifies

and deepens those values attained through human efforts. (Gutiérrez 1988, p. xvii)

Gustavo Gutiérrez, who opens his revised edition of *A Theology of Liberation* with these words, states that they express 'so well both the historical situation of liberation theology and the perspective of faith in which it interprets this situation' (ibid., p. xviii). He adds that the name and reality of 'liberation theology' came into existence at Chimbote, Peru, in July 1968, only a few months before Medellín. This perspective, then, provides the interpretative framework for the liberation theology movement. It also shows its consonance and probable roots in the Hegelian view of history, where the Spirit is at work within the dialectical struggles of humanity to bring into being the kingdom of God.

For the liberation theologians of the 1970s and 1980s this divine presence was especially manifest in the basic Christian communities which had grown up across the continent during the previous decade. During the 1970s it was estimated that there were some 40,000 of these, mostly in poor rural areas and on the outskirts of towns, co-ordinated by lay people and committed to celebration of the Word, shared prayer and mutual help, joining with others for the Eucharist when the priest visited the area.

> Social commitment is a feature which is found among them, but it does not always assume a specifically political line. Greater stress is laid on the concern of the communities to awaken people's awareness, leading them to make their own socio-political commitment, not in the name of the community but in the name of faith. (Marins 1979, p. 240)

Many groups were engaging in short courses on the Christian faith and, in the process, generating fresh and exciting perspectives on well-known passages of Scripture (see, for example, Cardenal 1976). The bishops at Medellín described the basic Christian communities as 'the initial cell of the Church structure and the source of evangelisation, and at the present time the primordial factor of human advancement and development' (ibid., p. 235).

Subsequently, of course, the Roman Catholic hierarchy under Pope John Paul II turned against this movement and tried to suppress it. Also, in situations of great oppression some adherents of the movement, such as Camillo Torres, aligned themselves very closely with military struggle against dictatorships, and this also blunted the impact of the movement. But through the witness of bishops like Heldar Camara (who rallied the movement with the statement that there was no point in feeding people the bread of life until they had enough bread for their stomachs), and of martyrs such as Archbishop Oscar Romero, its influence spread beyond Latin America. It was taken up with enthusiasm in other parts of the world. More recently Gutiérrez has cited Black, Hispanic, and Amerindian theologies in the United States, theologies arising in the complex contexts of Africa, Asia and the South Pacific, and especially 'the fruitful thinking of those who have adopted the feminist perspective', as examples of this widening influence (Gutiérrez 1988, p. xix). The civil rights movement in the United States, led by Martin Luther King, Jnr, and described in Chapter 1, provides a similar example of this kind of movement from an earlier decade.

The liberation theology of Latin America and other parts of the developing world therefore gave Enlightenment modern mission, with its belief in the possibility and need to build the kingdom of God on earth, a new lease of life. It showed that the churches could align themselves with certain historical forces, forces sometimes identified most clearly in the writings of Karl Marx. The people of God could stand alongside others who were also influenced by his perspective who were fighting for the material liberation of the poor and underprivileged of the world. The coming of the kingdom of God could be identified with the political and economic emancipation of such oppressed peoples and real steps taken toward its realization. (For discussion of current expression of liberation theology see Petrella 2006.)

Faith in the City

A different and influential example is the 1985 Church of England report *Faith in the City* and the subsequent movement to establish the Church Urban Fund. The report was a response to inner city riots, notably at Brixton, which made it clear that both church and nation needed to take a new look at the most deprived areas in the larger cities and at the recent growth of poverty.

In 1983 Robert Runcie, the archbishop of Canterbury, set up a high-powered commission, mostly of lay people, chaired by Sir Richard O'Brien, formerly Chairman of the government's Manpower Services Commission, to examine the situation and make recommendations. The report was published in December 1985 and was fiercely attacked by some Conservative politicians as a 'Marxist' document. In fact the Commission contained no Marxist and the report no Marxism. It was clear the government was unhappy to have attention drawn to a state of affairs about which it was at the time doing very little. Adrian Hastings comments that

> the report's analysis was in fact masterly. Most of its recommendations were directed to the church (a point its secular critics almost entirely overlooked: they attacked it as the work of a group of priests telling the government what to do. In fact it was far more a group of laity telling the church what to do). It led to the Church Urban Fund, to a new urban strategy and to a considerable improvement in morale among people working in this area. It provided a sense of direction, achievable goals and it generated a network of support, being followed by comparable local reports for Birmingham, Manchester and Leeds. It also almost certainly led to the government's greater concern for inner city areas as shown in the 1987 election, but it also showed that in regard to great human need at home as much as abroad the role of the church could still be of paramount importance if played with adequate competence. (Hastings 2001, pp. xxxvii–xxxviii)

While the commission would not have claimed to be building the kingdom on earth, its whole approach and its outcomes demonstrated a confidence and success in using rational and empirical investigation to provide a way forward for church and society. In particular it placed its trust in a panel of experts to discuss and agree the right way forward for building a better society in which there would especially be a significant improvement in the social conditions of the urban poor. In this rationality-based and progressivist view of Christian mission *Faith in the City* therefore provides a recent, striking and significant example of Enlightenment modern mission.

Summary of the Enlightenment modern Christian paradigm

Context
Scientific discovery, rationalism, industrialization, Romanticism.

Hierarchy of authorities
1. Reason/nature
2. Tradition
3. Scripture

Methodology
Rationalist: philosophically systematic.

Eschatology
The kingdom lies in the future but is being realized through human progress, e.g. scientific, psychological, artistic, working with the Spirit.

Christology
Incarnational: Jesus present among us (esp. as teacher and healer) as the pioneer of a new humanity which is gradually coming about.

Discipleship
To become conscious/enlightened/educated about this coming kingdom, and to work for its realization with others.

Mission of the Church
To be a committed agent of the kingdom, helping to build its presence in the world, esp. through education, medicine, artistic creativity.

Ministry
To professionally educate, medically heal, and develop local and national communities that conform to the coming kingdom.

Some examples
Hegel, W. Temple, liberation theology, *Faith in the City*.

Debate

> ### Galilean principles of the *missio Christi* (from p. 33)
>
> 1. Contemplative listening, which frames all ministry: listening to God, to other people, to oneself, especially in times of prayer and retreat.
>
> 2. Addressing society as a whole, at points where people live and work, including and especially the marginalized. This results in being received and accepted by some but rejected and opposed by others.
>
> 3. Pointing to the inaugurated yet still awaited kingdom, in word and in surprising saving deed (symbolic actions) which address the actual needs of people (both individual and structural); but without publicizing the wonders.
>
> 4. Calling for a personal response by all to the coming of this kingdom.
>
> 5. Doing all this through a collaborative team, who themselves are powerless and vulnerable and must suffer the consequences.

One response

1. Can it be said that contemplative listening frames the Enlightenment modern mission type? In one way the answer can be affirmative because the paradigm from which it comes was born in the patient and rigorous listening that were part of early scientific endeavour. Through the methodical attentiveness of scientists like Galileo and Newton great steps were taken, and so impressive were the results that a whole new way of viewing the world came about. This rigorous and methodical approach was then carried through into other areas of life and the Age of Reason, the Enlightenment, was inaugurated.

Enlightenment mission, in so far as it embraced and developed this kind of approach, can therefore be given a positive assessment against the first of the Galilean principles. However, the other side of the coin was that the elevation of human reason into the primary authority for guiding human living resulted in a gradual turning away from the transcendent and listening to God. With human beings now able to measure and assess the world around them without recourse to any outside authorities, what need was there for listening to the voice of the divine other? As the Enlightenment era progressed, and the influence of Christian philosophers such as Locke, Berkeley and Hegel gave way to the agnosticism of Darwin and the atheism of Marx, Nietzsche and Freud, the place of religious authority was increasingly questioned. The sacred came to be entirely replaced by the secular as the only realm that counted, and modernity in the twentieth century became fundamentally disinterested in religious concerns.

In a similar way it is possible to argue that Christian mission became more and more concerned with the physical and technical aspects of education, medicine and social reform, as witnessed in the building of great church-sponsored educational and medical institutions around the world, and less concerned with 'the other', whether human or divine. Consequently, it has been argued that Western missionaries lost a willingness to dialogue with those who were different from themselves, such as pagan and tribal peoples in other parts of the world or, indeed, with the unchurched sections of Western populations. Consequently the latter part of the twentieth century saw missionaries acquire a widespread notoriety for the way they imported Western culture, values and commerce into regions of the world where it was thoroughly inappropriate. While individual missionaries provided notable exceptions to the rule, and while a figure like William Temple exemplified great openness to the social, cultural and economic forces of his time, the Enlightenment modern mission type as a whole displayed an overriding confidence in the superiority of its message over that of other faiths and points of view. And while this sense of confidence was necessary in some contexts of acute poverty and suffering, in general terms it meant this type struggled to express the first Galilean principle.

2. It is important to acknowledge the universalism of the Enlightenment paradigm: it advocated the overturning of the old hierarchies of church and state in Europe and the recognition of the dignity and equality of every human being. Neither kings nor popes were to stipulate what people believe: there should be freedom of conscience and freedom of expression. Progress in science, technology and medicine was therefore to be offered to everyone throughout society, and not just to the old aristocratic elites. Within the churches this translated into an increasing concern for the education, housing, medical care and social security of every member of society. William Temple is a good example of this aspect of Enlightenment modern mission, with his tireless work to promote the

idea of the welfare state, which finally bore fruit after his death in the post-war Labour government of 1945–52. As far as the second Galilean principle is concerned, then, it is clear that this type of mission was fundamentally concerned with every member of society and especially the marginalized.

3. Hegel and his followers had a strong sense that the kingdom of God was coming about here on earth. The quotation from William Temple in 1917 (on p. 146) shows this belief continuing into the twentieth century: with great confidence it announces that we are living on the cusp of the kingdom's arrival and the march of progress has almost reached its conclusion. Similarly the liberation theology movement in Latin America in the 1970s had a powerful sense that it was riding the wave of an incoming social and political revolution. But what is missing with both is a recognition that for some people the life of the world is declining rather than progressing and that the onward march of Western civilization is part of the problem rather than the solution. In important respects the kingdom is *not* present and not about to be present. It can be argued that Enlightenment modern mission gives insufficient recognition to this dimension of eschatology: it is so full of confidence in what it is doing that it glosses over the voices and communities which speak in a different way. The third Galilean principle demands that mission points to a kingdom which is not yet seen and is still awaited, and again this mission type seems to fall short at this point.

However, when it comes to using deeds as well as words in its proclamation this type achieves a strong score. The medical as well as educational work of the churches over the last two centuries has been pioneering and extensive, reaching every continent and bringing health and education to millions of people. In many places the state has now assumed responsibility for this work but history should not be ignored and there should be proper recognition of the contribution of churches over the last two centuries.

4. Has the need for a personal response to mission been integral to Enlightenment modern mission? With its emphasis on education, medical care and social reform, this type concentrated on building medical and educational establishments and on political involvement and pressure. It can be argued that this kind of approach removed the necessity of its subjects making a personal commitment to what was happening, because its aim was improving the physical and mental rather than spiritual conditions in which they lived.

In a powerful passage in *Christianity Rediscovered* Vincent Donovan mounts this very argument, criticizing the extensive network of mission stations that the Roman Catholic Church had built across Tanzania. They had provided valuable education and medical care, but had failed to foster any kind of genuine commitment among the people they were serving: 'As of this month, in the seventh year of this mission's existence, there are no adult Masai practising Christians from Loliondo mission . . . up until this date no Catholic child, on leaving school, has continued to practise his religion, and there is no indication that any of the present students will do so . . .' (Donovan 1982, p. 15). Donovan believed that the Masai communities had been let down in the way they had been approached by the missionaries: they had not been given the genuine possibility of making a personal response to the gospel, and so he embarked on a completely different approach to mission, one that will be examined in the next chapter.

5. To what extent have representatives of this type of mission worked through collaborative teams, which are powerless and vulnerable and suffer the consequences of that vulnerability? There cannot be one answer to this question. With its emphasis on rationality, technique and expertise the Enlightenment tradition has had a history of disempowering those who are not seen as intelligent or as experts or to have mastered the relevant techniques. The Enlightenment replaced one set of hierarchies, based on ancestral privilege or ecclesiastical preferment, with another set, based on academic or technical achievement. The churches have been as susceptible to this as other parts of society, with their own entrenched clerical hierarchies based on the kinds of education that clergy have received.

Yet, on the other hand, the educational, medical and political work could never have achieved as much as it did without close co-operation between teams of highly committed people. Behind the great institutions and their charismatic leaders there have been teams of fellow-workers, providing the back-room administrative and personal support and doing the spadework to ensure the provision continued. This was certainly the case with William Temple, who not only relied on a close-knit group of committed staff, such as P. T. R. Kirk and members of the Industrial Christian Fellowship, but who embodied and developed the highly collaborative Christian Socialist tradition of the previous fifty years. It is even more the case with liberation theology, which is very explicit about the need to work with others and especially with the poor, not dictating what should happen but learning from and facilitating their struggle against oppression.

Conclusion

As with other types of mission, then, the Enlightenment modern type achieves a mixed score when it is assessed against Jesus' Galilean principles. It does not score highly with the first and the fourth principles, it achieves a mixed score with the second and the fifth principles, but does very well with the third. This is a better score than that of the medieval type, but not as good as that of the Reformation type. Does this mean it should be abandoned? Not in some contexts. Richard Gillett has recently argued for the continuing relevance and power of this mission type in the North American context where low-skilled and poor people, especially migrant workers, desperately need the kind of social and political intervention that it advocates (Gillett 2005). He argues, for example, that it was correct that a Catholic priest supported the right of Mexican migrant workers to join a union in a meat-packing factory in Nebraska and that this example should be followed in other places. Exploitation demands structural responses, and this mission type provides the theological resources to make such responses possible.

> **Discussion questions**
>
> Are there local contexts that you know where this type of mission may be just what is needed?
> What might the strengths and weaknesses of this type of mission be within your own home context?

Further reading

Bauckham, Richard (1995), *The Theology of Jürgen Moltmann*, T & T Clark
Bosch, David J. (1991), *Transforming Mission: Paradigm Shifts in Theology of Mission*, Orbis

Cardenal, Ernesto (1976), *The Gospel in Solentiname*, Orbis

Donovan, Vincent (1982), *Christianity Rediscovered: An Epistle from the Masai*, SCM Press

Faith in the City (1975), Archbishop of Canterbury's Commission in Urban Priority Areas, Church House Publishing

Gillett, Richard W. (2005), *The New Globalization: Reclaiming the Lost Ground of our Christian Tradition*, Pilgrim Press

Grimley, Matthew (2004), *Citizenship, Community and the Church of England: Liberal Anglican Theories of the State between the Wars*, Oxford University Press

Gutiérrez, Gustavo (1988), *A Theology of Liberation*, revised edition, SCM Press

Hastings, Adrian (2001), *A History of English Christianity 1920–2000*, SCM Press

Hegel, G. W. F. (1975), *Lectures on the Philosophy of World History*, with introduction by Duncan Forbes, Cambridge University Press

Hodgson, Peter C. (2005), *Hegel and Christian Theology: A Reading of the Lectures on the Philosophy of Religion*, Oxford University Press

Jenkins, David (1981), 'Christianity, Social Order, and the Story of the World', in *Theology*, SPCK, pp. 321–4

Kent, John (1992), *William Temple: Church, State and Society in Britain 1880–1950*, Cambridge University Press

Küng, Hans (1995), *Christianity: Its Essence and History*, SCM Press

Marins, José (1979), 'Basic Ecclesial Communities in Latin America', *International Review of Mission*, vol. 68, WCC

Moltmann, Jürgen (1967), *Theology of Hope: On the Ground and Implications of a Christian Eschatology*, SCM Press

Pannenberg, Wolfhart (1967), 'Revelation as History', in C. T. McIntyre, ed., *God, History and Historians* (1977), Oxford University Press

Petrella, Ivan (2006), *The Future of Liberation Theology: An Argument and Manifesto*, SCM Press

Reardon, Bernard M. G. (1985), *Religion in the Age of Romanticism: Studies in Early Nineteenth Century Thought*, Cambridge University Press

Singer, Peter (1983), *Hegel*, Oxford University Press

Spencer, Stephen (2001), *William Temple: A Calling to Prophecy*, SPCK

Stott, John (1986), *Christian Mission in the Modern World*, Kingsway

Temple, William (1917), *Mens Creatrix*, Macmillan

Temple, William (1976), *Christianity and Social Order*, new edition, Shepheard-Walwyn and SPCK, with Foreword by Edward Heath

Vatican Council II: The Basic Sixteen Documents (1996), ed. Austin Flannery OP, Dominican Publications

10

Finding Hope in Local Communities Mission within Postmodernity

In *Christianity Rediscovered* Vincent Donovan presents a now famous picture of the way he went to Masai villages in East Africa not to offer education in schools, or medical care, or any kind of political strategy to improve the material conditions of their lives. Nor did he go to evangelize the Masai in any sense in which that word is normally used, because he was never sure what he was going to say to them before he arrived. Instead he did something different and highly significant in the development of mission:

> Each day, in that brisk, early morning hour, still unheated by the equatorial sun, there in the Masai highlands, with the background of the lowing cattle, as I stood waiting for them to gather, I was conscious of the knot in my stomach, wondering if this were the day it would all blow up in my face, with Christianity being utterly rejected by these sons of the plains. Many is the time in that lonely, nomadic setting that I wished I were back in the comfortable company of familiar and acquiescent Christians.
>
> I had to tell them that very first day, when they had all gathered, that I had come to talk about, and deal only with, God. (Donovan 1982, p. 24)

The talk was not just his own talk. The Masai villagers had their own questions and answers. In his book Donovan presents an account of a genuine dialogue between two parties, a dialogue with surprising results:

> Going back and forth among these pagan communities week by week, I soon realized that not one week would go by without some surprising rejoinder or reaction or revelation from these Masai. My education was beginning in earnest.
>
> The process followed was simple. I would mention a religious theme or thought and ask to hear their opinion on it, and then I would tell them what I believed on the same subject, a belief I had come eight thousand miles to share with them. I have done pastoral and social work in America and Africa, and have taught in a major seminary. But I have never been so tested in my life as by these pagan sons and daughters of the plain. (ibid., p. 41)

This was not, then, a one-way street for mission: there was significant traffic in both directions. Donovan was bringing the gospel to share with the Masai, but the language and idioms open to him were those of the Masai, and these were forcing him to rethink and recast his understanding of that gospel.

Christianity Rediscovered propels us into a theological world strikingly and disturbingly different from those of the Reformation and Enlightenment. This chapter will explore the roots of this world, its classical expression in some mid-twentieth-century theologians, and some exciting contemporary expressions.

Background

Cultural trends: from modernity to postmodernity

The roots of this new theological world or paradigm partly lie in the collapse of Enlightenment aspirations. Historians describe how the rise of industrialization, first in the north of England and then across northern Europe, was followed in the nineteenth century by European commercial expansion around the world, carrying Western culture, philosophy and education to many points across the globe. The Age of Reason became the colonial age of empire in which the European powers harnessed technology and industrialization for the scramble for global domination. The next step along this road was war between the competing European powers. Many commentators see the First World War as the outcome of the Enlightenment era, where the so-called enlightened European powers proceeded to kill a whole generation of their young men on the battlefields with their new-found technology. These desperate events were followed by the Versailles Treaty, the humiliation of Germany and the rise of Nazism, and then, of course, the Holocaust, the Second World War and the dropping of the atomic bombs on Hiroshima and Nagasaki. These unparalleled events have been seen by some as the dark conclusion of the Enlightenment's belief in the power of humanity to perfect itself. For many they undermined belief in the existence of human progress founded on reason and technology. And while technology has continued to develop with great speed in the twentieth century, it is now regarded with wariness by many in the West: since the Second World War there have arisen a number of anti-technology movements, such as opposition to the atomic bomb, to modernist civic developments and to genetic engineering.

A second key development in this period has been mass immigration into Western societies from the Indian sub-continent, Africa and central Asia. This has resulted in the rise of pluralist societies in Europe, with different religions, cultures, languages and customs rubbing shoulders with each other in most of the larger European cities. And this has included the arrival of not only non-Christian religions but Pentecostalist forms of Christianity from the southern hemisphere (see Jenkins 2002).

In the latter part of the twentieth century these two developments gave rise to a new way of relativistic thinking in Western culture, at least in the urban centres. This is often called 'postmodernism' and has led some commentators to describe the end of the twentieth and the beginning of the twenty-first centuries as the start of a new era, the postmodern era. According to Michael Gallagher in *Clashing Symbols* (Gallagher 2003) it can be seen as having two forms, a philosophical movement which is very critical of what it replaces, which he calls *postmodernism*, and a broader and more open cultural movement which he terms *postmodernity*.

Postmodernism was born in the poststructuralist philosophy of French literary critics such as Jacques Derrida (1930–2005), Michel Foucault (1926–84) and Jean François Lyotard (1924–98). A text which summed up the aim of the movement was Lyotard's *The Postmodern Condition* of 1979. He described post-modernism as 'the deconstruction of the metanarratives of modernity'. A meta-narrative was any attempt to provide an overarching account of reality, which included not only the traditional grand narratives of religion but, significantly, modernist metanarratives in the works of Adam Smith, Kant, Hegel, Marx, Freud, and any others who claimed to provide systems of religious, political, economic or cultural ideas. Gallagher helpfully summarizes the key beliefs of *postmodernism*, which he terms its 10 Commandments, indicating its didactic nature. These show the way it was a deliberate attempt to reject Enlightenment values and aspirations: 'Thou shalt not worship reason'; 'Thou shalt not believe in history'; 'Thou shalt not hope in progress'; 'Thou shalt not tell meta-stories'; 'Thou shalt not focus on the self'; 'Thou shalt not agonise about values'; 'Thou shalt not trust institutions'; 'Thou shalt not bother about God'; 'Thou shalt not live for productivity alone'; 'Thou shalt not seek uniformity' (Gallagher 2003, pp. 100–3). Instead, in Lyotard's terms, it is necessary to accept the 'incommensurability' of various forms of discourse and the 'difference' between them, to be sensitive to the breakdowns in communications that take place between people, and to develop a better understanding of them.

Gallagher describes *postmodernity*, on the other hand, as more open and creative and something that

> is a new sensibility that aims at wholeness. It sees modernity as having caused an abyss between the rational and the subjective aspects of humanity – by developing both dimensions in isolation from one another. Postmodernity as sensibility is groping towards forms of life that bridge these divisions . . . there is . . . a different searching beyond the old certitudes, including a new willingness to revisit the despised zones of the spiritual and religious as roots of our healing. (2003, p. 108)

In this movement he sees therefore a 'humbler searching' with an openness to ecological and feminist concerns as well as to the spiritual. It draws on the imagination and on a social commitment to bring healing to old wounds and to liberate different zones of life (p. 107).

A theological revolution

In tandem with these traumatic social and cultural events there has been an unfolding theological revolution. It was foreshadowed at a gathering of theologians at Eisenach in Germany in 1896. Ernst Troeltsch (1865–1923), a newly appointed professor who would later help to institute the modern discipline of sociology of religion, sprang to the rostrum and uttered some disturbing words: 'Gentlemen, everything is tottering' (quoted in Stuart Hughes 1979, p. 230). This was a dramatic summary of an argument he presented in his article 'The Crisis of Historicism'. Up to that point he had been a scholar who, typical of his age (and influenced by the Hegelians), looked to the history of human development for the basis of values. He had been 'convinced that knowledge and values could only be won from history . . . history became the only way to gain true knowledge and the historical approach constituted the most significant advancement of the modern spirit'. And he believed that even though this knowledge and these values were 'relative to specific historical situations, [they] reflected an absolute truth' (Iggers 1968, p. 188). But now, at Eisenach and in his article, Troeltsch stated that historical study did *not* give us understanding. Rather, it had undermined 'all firm norms and ideals of human existence . . . Politics, law, morality, religion and art were all dissolved in the stream of history and became comprehensible only as parts of specific historical developments.' He now believed the modern study of history had 'shattered our ethical systems' and the belief in humanitarian progress (ibid., p. 189).

Karl Barth, already introduced on p. 10, began his theological reflection within this setting of crisis. He had also grown up within the liberal historicism which was predominant in Protestant theology in the nineteenth and early twentieth centuries. His teachers Adolf von Harnack (Berlin) and Wilhelm Herrman (Marburg) were typical representatives and saw religion as concerned with the cultivation of people's spiritual faculties. They believed humanity might achieve union with the divine: it had the capacity to gradually lead itself to God. Barth led a revolt against this way of thinking. He may be called the first clear exponent of a new theological paradigm which broke radically with an Enlightenment approach to theology (see Küng 1995, pp. 165–6).

This began to happen when Karl Barth became the pastor of the industrial town of Safenwil from 1911. He saw the poverty of the victims of industrial capitalism and understood that the progress of civilization had not brought them freedom but oppression. He realized that his training, premised on such progress, had given him nothing to say to these people: at the same time as he read and preached on the Scriptures he found in the Bible a 'strange new world', a reality to be understood only by inhabiting it, a world defined not by our quest for God but by God's coming to us (Jenson 1997, p. 21).

During the First World War Barth was aware of the slaughter on the battlefields and the 'suicide' of European liberal culture, and this strengthened his sense of alienation from contemporary theology. He heard his own teachers call for loyalty above all to the Kaiser and the Fatherland! Barth became a questioner, an outsider, a left-winger.

He lectured, wrote papers and made two attempts to write a commentary on Paul's letter to the Romans. The second edition was published in 1922 and was written as a dialogue with the reader. It is 'a direct assault on the reader: it seeks not to inform but to transform' (Jenson 1997, p. 26): its point is to question and unnerve the reader so that he or she questions their liberal assumptions about religion and is thrown back *onto God* to receive from his grace, which it saw as eternity breaking into time, a reality with an 'infinite qualitative difference' (Kierkegaard, quoted by Barth, in Jenson 1997, p. 26).

The second edition of *Romans* achieved instant celebrity: it became the rallying point for a new generation of Protestant pastors and teachers and Barth's career as a professional theologian was now under way. He lectured at Göttingen, Münster and, from 1930, at Bonn, where he became the theological leader of the 'confessing' resistance to Hitler's attempt to take over control of the German evangelical church. He was the chief drafter of the Confessing Movement's 'Barmen Declaration' (see Bradstock and Rowland 2002, ch. 37). This resulted in his being banned from teaching in Germany in 1935. He returned to Switzerland and taught at Basel for the rest of his life, writing and publishing the *Church Dogmatics* between 1932 and 1967 and coming to play with relish the role of the Church's most famous and controversial theologian.

Barth builds his theology on the work of Friedrich Schleiermacher (1768–1834), often called the father of modern theology, but he radically inverts it. Schleiermacher began his theology with an analysis of human existence, showing that religion is a necessary component of complete personal life. The direction in which he moved was from nature or natural theology as the basis for Christian theology, towards Christ and Christianity, letting the former define the question that the latter must answer.

Barth turned this on its head:

> Instead of interpreting Christianity by the general character and function of religion, he interprets religion, including Christian religion, by Christianity's differentiating specificity. Instead of analyzing human existence, in order then to inquire after Christ's contribution to the religious aspect, he analyzes Christ's existence, in order then to inquire after our religion's place therein. (Jenson 1997, p. 25)

Christ's revelation is primary, for Barth: everything else must be seen in the light of that. So, in response to his fellow theologian Emil Brunner's 'yes' to the possibility of natural theology, he proclaimed a loud and famous 'no' to the very idea of doing it. Instead, the discipline of theology must have Christ's life, death and resurrection, or *the Christ event* as Barth called it, as its beginning, middle and end. Theology consists in tracing the significance of this event for every aspect of life. Christ the Word of God reveals the truth of all things. Hence Barth's theology, especially the 14 volumes (8,000 pages) of his *Church Dogmatics*, is a work of Christology. It begins with the doctrine of the Word of God, which sets out the basics of his position, concentrating on the priority of the revelation of the Word of God over everything else. Barth assumes God has decisively revealed himself in Christ, and his task as a theologian is to draw out the meaning of this for the Christian community. He does not begin his theology with general and abstract philosophical arguments about 'the ground of being' or 'the feeling of absolute dependence', as nineteenth-century theologians tended to do. He begins with God as revealed by Christ, in his birth, work, crucifixion and resurrection. Then in the second volume, when he addresses the doctrine of God, he brings the doctrine of the Trinity to centre stage, because he sees the nature of God *as defined by* the interrelations of the Son and Holy Spirit with the Father: 'It is from Barth that twentieth-century theology has relearned that this doctrine has and must have explanatory and regulatory use in the whole of theology, that it is not a separate puzzle to be solved but the framework within which all theology's puzzles are to be solved' (Jenson 1997, p. 31).

Even when Barth explores the doctrine of creation he relates it to Christ. He describes God's work in creating the world as being about setting in place the right conditions for the revelation of his Son. This is one of his most original contributions to theology. Then, when he comes to look at the person and work of Christ, he does this over four massive volumes in his 'Doctrine of Reconciliation'.

Church Dogmatics is not a deductive piece of work, building a logical argument by moving on from one point to the next. Rather each volume stands in its own right as a meditation upon the way Christ defines and saves human life. It is possible to pick up and read any of the volumes without having read any of the others before.

Barth was first misunderstood and rejected, especially in Britain and North America: his theology was labelled as 'neo-orthodoxy' and dismissed as reactionary. But now he is recognized as the pioneer of an approach to theology which is no longer dependent on philosophy or the study of history and has found its authority in a transcendent revelation, the Word of God found in the Christ event. In different language, he has allowed the Church to see that the kingdom of God is not built through human effort and the progress of civilization (as Hegel and his successors argued) but comes from God, as his gracious gift, as a transcendent reality breaking into the corruption and failures of human life. In an age which has witnessed the collapse of Enlightenment hopes in humanity's ability to improve itself, Barth has provided alternative grounds for hope.

Mission within postmodernity

The traumas of the twentieth century and the rise of a pluralist and relativist culture cut the ground from Enlightenment mission, because they showed that the Church had no reason to think that its major educational and health care projects would usher in the kingdom of God. Despite all the progress in spreading the institutions of Christianity around the world in the nineteenth century, the twentieth century was arguably the most bloody and dehumanizing in history. While the work of church schools, hospitals and political involvement undoubtedly improved the physical well-being of many people, such work had not resolved or begun to resolve the ultimate issues and questions of the reign of God.

Barth had seen that these issues and questions could only be resolved by God himself: it was the divine revelation in Christ that provided the answer to the questions of humanity. This insight had radical consequences for the Church's understanding of mission. We have already seen Barth's impact at the

Brandenburg Missionary Conference of 1932 and the Willingen Conference of the International Missionary Council in 1952 (Chapter 2). Barth was the key figure behind the coining of the phrase *missio Dei* as a summary of mission's dependence on the initiative and sustenance of God himself. Mission was not to be seen as one of humanity's building projects, carried forward by its own strength and reason, but as a divine movement in which the Church was privileged to participate.

But what, in practical terms, was the response of the Christian community to be? What was the role of the Church within this bracing context?

It was one of Barth's students who began to map out the answer. Dietrich Bonhoeffer (1906–45), a German Lutheran theologian and pastor who resisted the Nazis and was put to death by them, has been described as 'the architect' of a new way of understanding the mission of the Church (Bosch 1991, p. 375). He did this in his writings and his life, especially from his prison cell before he was executed. He described some of the implications for Christians who take the *otherness* of God's grace and mission seriously. With Barth he saw that the foundation of faith, mission, the Church and theology is not human enquiry, reason or science but God's revelation in Jesus Christ. The only true allegiance was to Christ as Lord. This was why he joined Barth in the German Confessing Church in 1934 as it broke away from the German National Church over its allegiance to Hitler. But Bonhoeffer went beyond Barth in emphasizing the importance of living within the community of the Church as a way of receiving and living out this revelation. He believed that the Christian community was the concrete presence of Christ in the world and needed to be valued and nurtured as such (his first book was on these themes, *Sanctorum Communio*, published in 1930, as was his *Life Together* of 1937). He therefore introduced a Catholic emphasis on the corporate life of the Church into a Barthian outlook.

Bonhoeffer also saw that the Christian life if taken seriously is no easy matter. He opposed what he called the offering of cheap grace by the established churches to their members. In his book *The Cost of Discipleship* he described the costly nature of following Christ, a way of service rather than domination.

Between 1934 and 1945 Bonhoeffer experienced the reality of this cost. He was banned from teaching, harassed by the authorities, left Germany and then bravely returned at the outbreak of the war to stand by his people. His defiant opposition, including his association with the group of people who tried to assassinate Hitler, led to his arrest and eventually his execution.

His writings and especially his *Letters and Papers from Prison* help to articulate a theology of mission implicit in the witness of his life. He moved away from seeing God as an almighty fixer, who controls his creation through the power and domination of the Church. He saw the modern era, which he called 'man's coming of age', as one in which humanity had discovered how to live life without reference to God and one which had therefore marginalized him. This, though, was not necessarily a bad thing: 'God allows himself to be edged out of the world and on to the cross. God is weak and powerless in the world, and that is exactly the way, the only way, in which he can be with us and help us' (Bonhoeffer 1959, p. 122). This has implications for discipleship:

> Man is challenged to participate in the sufferings of God at the hands of a godless world. He must therefore plunge himself into the life of a godless world, without attempting to gloss over its ungodliness with a veneer of religion or trying to transfigure it. He must live a 'Worldly' life and so participate in the suffering of God . . . It is not some religious act which makes a Christian what he is, but participation in the suffering of God in the life of the world . . . (ibid., pp. 122–3)

In an outline for a book at the end of the *Letters and Papers* he describes what this means for the mission of the Church:

> The Church is her true self only when she exists for humanity. As a fresh start she should give away all her endowments to the poor and needy. The clergy should live solely on the free-will offerings of their congregations, or possibly engage in some secular calling. She must take part in the social life of the world, not lording it over men, but helping and serving them. She must tell men, whatever their calling, what it means to live in Christ, to exist for others. (p. 166)

Christian mission, then, is about the Church laying aside its own power and becoming open and vulnerable to the world, giving itself to serving the needs of others, locating itself where they live and only then, finally, seeking to communicate the meaning of the gospel: Christian mission is all about witness out of a prior vulnerability.

Bonhoeffer's *Letters and Papers* was published in German in 1951 and in

English in 1953. It would take another decade for its challenges to become widely known and accepted. But its influence spread in the 1960s and eventually Bonhoeffer, as already mentioned, would come to be described as 'the architect' of this way of viewing the mission of the Church (see further Dulles 1988, pp. 94–5).

Case study: Vincent Donovan and the Masai

The 1960s was also the decade in which Vincent Donovan, a Roman Catholic missionary priest, began his work among the Masai people of Tanzania. While he was not directly influenced by Bonhoeffer, the approach to mission that developed out of his work is one that vividly puts into practice the principles Bonhoeffer was describing.

His approach to mission, significantly, had as its premise the failure of the institutional Church through its educational, medical and ecclesial bodies to make any headway in converting the Masai people. The work of the mission station to which he was posted was entirely concerned with its school and hospital. The priests visited the homesteads where the people lived to recruit for the school but the subject of God was never mentioned. Donovan asked permission from his bishop to adopt a different approach. He wanted to cut himself off

> from the hospital and schools as well as the socializing with them – and just go and talk to them about God and the Christian message . . . I want to go to the Masai on daily safaris – unencumbered with the burden of selling them our school system, or begging for their children for our schools, or carrying their sick, or giving them medicine. Outside of this, I have no theory, no plan, no strategy, no gimmicks – no idea of what will come. I feel rather naked. I will begin as soon as possible. (Donovan 1982, pp. 15–16)

With great eloquence Donovan then describes the encounters he had with different Masai villagers, his own vulnerability and the specific nature of what he wanted to talk about. The quotation at the start of this chapter described the knot in his stomach that preceded each encounter and how he had come to talk about, and deal only with, God.

The correlation with Bonhoeffer's vision of the vulnerable Church is striking.

Donovan was coming among the Masai in a way in which he laid himself open to rejection: he was genuinely offering himself to this indigenous community. What is also important is the element of real dialogue in Donovan's approach to the Masai, which was also described in the quotation above on how his education began in earnest when he entered into dialogue with the Masai.

This was not, we noted, a one-way street for mission: there was significant traffic going in both directions. Donovan was bringing the gospel to share with the Masai, but the language and idioms open to him were those of the Masai, and these were forcing him to rethink and recast his understanding of that gospel. One good example of this comes from near the end of his time with the Masai when he asked them, 'by what name would you refer to me in the job or role that I perform in your Christian community, even in the temporary way I do it, until one of you is ready to take over that job?' He was asking them to find a word in their own language which would describe the missionary service he had provided. They discussed many words, rejecting the equivalent of doctor, chief, rich one, even shepherd (because there were good and bad shepherds in their community). They chose instead a role that had no connection with their pagan religious practices:

> He was a man present to every community who was interested in all the flocks of the community and essential to the life of the community and interested in all phases of that life. He was a man to whom anyone could turn for special difficulties and help. It was amazing to me that such a man, and others like him, were found in pagan communities like the Masai. They were called *ilaretok* and represented an extraordinary aspect of pagan life. The word literally means helpers, yet it carries with it all the overtones and connotations of servants. They were helpers or servants of the community. That is the concept these people chose to represent what they understood of the function of the Christian priest. I conducted this inquiry in other sections of the mission area among other Christian elders, geographically unrelated to the first elders, and in each case they made the same choice and came up with the very same word. (Donovan 1982, pp. 157–8)

This is important because it shows how the Masai were influencing and re-forming Donovan's own understanding of Christianity. He had set out with the assumption that his evangelism would bring the reality of the Christian faith *to* them. This passage shows that something more complex and interesting had taken place, a two-way dialogue in which a new form of Christianity had been brought to life.

The West African scholar Lamin Sanneh has written an acclaimed study of this kind of dialogue. He traces what he calls the vernacular principle at work within it. Through many examples he shows that missionary preaching changed the missionaries as much as their audience:

> The central premise of missionary preaching is also a most acute source of irony. Many missionaries assumed that Africans had not heard of God and that it was the task of mission to remedy this defect. In practical terms, however, missionaries started by inquiring among the people what names and concepts for God existed, and having established such fundamental points of contact, they proceeded to adopt local vocabulary to preach the gospel.

Sanneh then observes,

> This field method of adopting the vernacular came to diverge sharply from the ideology of mission. After all, it turns out, Africans had heard of God, described God most eloquently, and maintained towards God proper attitudes of reverence, worship, and sacrifice . . . Consequently, however much mission tried to suppress local populations, the issue of the vernacular helped to undermine its foreign character. (Sanneh 1989, p. 159)

Sanneh goes on to illustrate this point with the example of living with pluralism. Western missionaries had arrived in Africa believing in a jealous God who forbade worship of other deities. But when he or she started to use the local vernacular name for God, the audience heard the missionary talking about the g/God they already knew.

> The God of the ancestors was accordingly assimilated into the Yahweh of ancient Israel and 'the God and Father of our Lord Jesus Christ.' . . . The exclusive notion of Western Christianity was replaced with the inclusive rule of African religions, an inclusiveness that helped deepen the pluralist ethos of the gospel. By embarking on translation, missionaries stimulated this ethos, thus helping to lay the foundation for a remarkable stage in the religious evolution of African communities. (ibid., pp. 159–60)

In all of this something new was being formed, neither traditional African religion nor classical Western Christianity, but an original expression of the faith for that local context. The difference between Vincent Donovan and the missionaries that Sanneh describes is that Donovan became aware of this process as it was happening and welcomed it. His costly embracing of the vernacular principle shows his adoption of a different understanding of mission, one that could be called post-missionary or postmodern. It is one that has radical implications for the transformation of Christianity in new contexts. But, on the other hand, Donovan's account of the Masai's faith, such as their identification of ministry with servanthood seen above, shows deep continuities as well.

One further theme should be highlighted from Donovan's great book, the rediscovery of God's agency at work through the whole process, the rediscovery of the *missio Dei* that can make the same thing happen elsewhere and thereby inspires hope. Donovan describes how one of the Masai elders had not been very happy with the word that Donovan had used to translate the word 'faith': the Masai word meant literally 'to agree to'. The elder said that

> 'to believe' like that was similar to a white hunter shooting an animal with his gun from a great distance. Only his eyes and his fingers took part in the act. We should find another word. He said that for a man really to believe is like a lion going after its prey. His nose and eyes and ears pick up the prey. His legs give him the speed to catch it. All the power of his body is involved in the terrible death leap and single blow to the neck with the front paw, the blow that actually kills. And as the animal goes down the lion envelops it in his arms (Africans refer to the front legs of an animal as its arms), pulls it to himself, and makes it part of himself. This is the way a lion kills. This is the way a man believes. This is what faith is.

Donovan looked at the elder in silence and amazement. But his wise old teacher was not finished yet:

> 'We did not search you out, Padri,' he said to me. 'We did not even want you to come to us. You searched us out. You followed us away from your house into the bush, into the plains, into the steppes where our cattle are, into the hills where we take our cattle for water, into our villages, into our homes. You told us of the High God, how we must search for him, even leave our land

and our people to find him. But we have not done this. We have not left our land. We have not searched for him. He has searched for us. He has searched *us* out and found us. All the time we think we are the lion. In the end, the lion is God.' (Donovan 1982, p. 63)

Donovan adds that his own role as a herald of the gospel was only 'a small part of the mission of God to the world . . . [which is] the immeasurably greater plan of the relentless, pursuing God whose will on the world would not be thwarted. The lion is God' (p. 64).

Other recent expressions

The common theme found in Bonhoeffer and Donovan is of the Church laying aside its power and wealth and becoming vulnerable to the local community, listening before witnessing, changing and being changed by the encounter. Both describe the humility that is needed in the missionary, and the risk that their mission could fail to hand on the gospel. Donovan also conveys the creativity and hopefulness of this type of mission in the way that his audience not only heard the gospel but created a new and dynamic embodiment of it. Lamin Sanneh has identified the vernacular principle as responsible for this creativity. (Andrew Walls has described this kind of process as the translation principle in Christian history: see Walls 1996, ch. 3.)

This open-ended approach to mission has been expressed in an increasing number of places in the latter part of the twentieth century, especially as migration has resulted in people of different faiths increasingly living side by side with each other, and the churches have had to enter into dialogue with Muslims, Hindus, Sikhs and Buddhists (among others). This has taken place at every level, though not usually under the heading of 'mission' (see, for example, Wingate 2005). However, official church documents have recognized the place of dialogue within Christian mission. Bevans and Schroeder provide the following example from the Secretariat for Non-Christians of the Roman Catholic Church:

Dialogue is . . . the norm and necessary manner of every form of Christian mission, as well as of every aspect of it, whether one speaks of simple presence

and witness, service or direct proclamation. Any sense of mission not perme-
ated by such a dialogical spirit would go against the demands of true humanity and against the teachings of the Gospel. (In Bevans and Schroeder 2004,
p. 378)

There is also widespread recognition that the concept of dialogue does not
rule out witness to the gospel (keeping in play the revealed theology of Karl
Barth and others). This was dramatically affirmed by the World Council of
Churches at its assembly in Nairobi in 1975. The subsequent *Guidelines on
Dialogue* express the point eloquently:

we do not see dialogue and the giving of witness as standing in any contradiction to one another. Indeed, as Christians enter dialogue with their commitment to Jesus Christ, time and again the relationship of dialogue gives
opportunity for authentic witness. Thus to member churches of the WCC we
feel able with integrity to commend the way of dialogue as one in which Jesus
Christ can be confessed in the world today; at the same time we feel able with
integrity to assure our partners in dialogue that we come not as manipulators
but as genuine fellow-pilgrims, to speak with them of what we believe God to
have done in Jesus Christ who has gone before us, but whom we seek to meet
anew in dialogue. (World Council of Churches 1979)

This dialogue and witness/proclamation properly enter into a dialectic with
each other, as Bosch affirms:

we do not have all the answers and are prepared to live within the framework
of penultimate knowledge, that we regard our involvement in dialogue and
mission as an adventure, are prepared to take risks, and are anticipating sur-
prises as the Spirit guides us into fuller understanding. This is not opting for
agnosticism, but for humility. It is, however, a bold humility – or a humble
boldness. We know only in part, but we do know. And we believe that the
faith we profess is both true and just, and should be proclaimed. (Bosch 1991,
p. 489)

Emerging churches

A clear and contemporary example of this dialectic of dialogue and witness is the 'emerging church' movement, which is made up of a diverse but increasing number of recently founded church communities in North America and Britain that share a number of practices. The term 'emerging church' was coined by Karen Ward in 2000 to describe 'what is coming to the surface. It is new, unformed, still happening, emerging' (Ward, in Gibbs and Bolger 2006, p. 321). Most of these churches are small, consisting of independent groups of fewer than thirty people, or clusters of house groups with up to one hundred (see Healey and Hinton 2005 for descriptions of other similar small Christian communities around the world). Eddie Gibbs and Ryan Bolger provide the following introductory definition: 'emerging churches are missional communities arising from within postmodern culture and consisting of followers of Jesus who are seeking to be faithful in their place and time' (Gibbs and Bolger 2006, p. 28). This definition immediately shows that these churches have much in common with Bonhoeffer and Donovan: they are firmly located within the culture that they serve, rather than within some other ecclesial culture, seeking to live faithfully the way of Jesus out of that context. They creatively relate to what Gallagher termed *postmodernity* as opposed to *postmodernism*, which rejected religion (see above p. 163).

Gibbs and Bolger have conducted extensive research into the movement, spending five years collecting data in both the US and the UK and interviewing 50 church leaders, mostly under the age of 40. They 'identified patterns most prevalent in churches that take culture, specifically postmodern culture, seriously. Nine practices are common to each emerging church. Each emerging church, however, does possess three core practices. The other six practices are derivative of these three core practices' (Gibbs and Bolger 2006, p. 43). The three core practices are (1) identifying with the life of Jesus (understood as the life he lived before he was put to death, involving welcoming the outcast, hosting the stranger, challenging the political authorities by creating an alternative community); (2) transforming secular space, in the same way that postmodernity calls into question the separation of sacred and secular: emerging churches work within the secular for its sacralization, making all life sacred; (3) living as community within all realms of the life of their members, not just within a Sunday morning meeting: they function more as extended families than as affinity groups.

Out of these three core practices six other practices have arisen: (4) they are glad to welcome the stranger into the community; (5) they serve the needy with generosity, wanting to know the poor and be known by them; (6) they want everyone to participate in worship and other activities as producers rather than just as recipients; (7) they seek to be creative in worship and life together, reflecting the creativity of God; (8) they exercise decentralized leadership through the body as a whole, rather than having individual leaders set over the community; (9) they merge ancient and contemporary spiritualities, both corporate and personal.

Gibbs and Bolger also present the stories of many of these churches and of the people who help lead them. These stories bring the analysis to life and highlight some of the key features. One of the threads running through many of the stories is the element of exploration, risk and vulnerability in the emergence of these churches. Dwight Friesen of 'Quest' in Seattle shows the same kind of vulnerability and creativity found in Donovan's missionary work. He recounts how his own ambition to be the pastor of a large and thriving 'mega-church' had to give way to a more modest vocation of helping to lead a church community in which genuine relationships between people were valued above all else: 'I felt like I was dying, dying to the idea of the megachurch pastor, which seemed to me now as though it would be abusive to those who came. This was a time of serious soul searching. "If I am not that, then who am I?" I asked myself, for now I was faced with an invitation to labor in obscurity. I felt devastated.' He then reports that he 'felt a loss of security in who I was in relationship to Christ. I felt adrift. Speaking at our gatherings, I spoke more of doubt than of certainty. But opening up with my doubts and concerns freed others to do the same.' And out of this insecurity came a new vocation for his church: 'Our biggest ministry gives hope to those who have given up on church. We experience divine hope in our community by "being present in one another." We have a value that says, "We don't know for sure, but we sense God is calling us"' (ibid., pp. 271–2).

Another of the stories demonstrates the way emerging churches are embedded in postmodern culture (in much the same way that Donovan's Masai churches were part and parcel of Masai culture):

Visions (York, UK) worked for clubs on Friday nights, providing visuals for local promoters, and had worship on Sunday nights. From an integrity standpoint, they would not do anything at the club on Friday that they would not do in church on Sunday. Their life in the world must remain consistent with their faith commitment. Correspondingly, they would not do anything on Sunday that they would not do at the club on Friday – their faith had to be expressed in ways that was native to the culture around them. Living in the culture as a local, and yet pointing to One beyond the local, helps keep the emerging churches' worlds intact. (Sue Wallace, in ibid., p. 75)

Gibbs and Bolger comment that

When worship and witness are in sync, as with Visions, it creates a 24–7 spiritual life for their participants, overcoming the 'secular' aspects of their lives with reminders of God. Sue Wallace . . . explains, 'The reason we embrace culture in worship is not only to make the place feel like "home" to those coming into it from the outside world, but also to make us take our worship from our church space into our world. When you are in a shop or a pub, and you hear a track that has been used in church, it forges connections and makes you think about God.' When we bring our own culture to God in worship, then that experience extends to our daily lives when we are away from the community. These 'secular' worship expressions become reminders and clues of God everywhere. (pp. 75–6)

This shows that behind emerging churches is a strong sense of the prior mission of God in the world, the *missio Dei* highlighted by Karl Barth. Steve Collins expresses the same idea in different language: 'It's funny how we talk of "bringing things to God" – like he wasn't there all the time. What we're really doing is bringing our attention to bear on the relation between things and God that already exists, and maybe making a few conscious adjustments to our own place in it' (ibid., p. 217).

This strong sense of the *missio Dei* has even led some of the leaders to renounce traditional evangelism altogether:

I no longer believe in evangelism. To be postevangelism is to live our lives in Christ without a strategy but with the compassion and the servant posture of Jesus Christ. We do not do evangelism or have a mission. The Holy Spirit is the evangelist, and the mission belongs to God. What we do is simply live our lives publicly as a community in the way of Jesus Christ, and when people inquire as to why we live this way, we share with them an account of the hope within us. We are to love one another, and that creates its own attraction. Taking care of the sick and the needy creates all the evangelism we need. (Karen Ward, in ibid., p. 135)

This demonstrates the distinctiveness of the postmodern approach to mission: it is not centred, as in the Enlightenment modern type, on human projects for educational, medical and political progress; nor is it centred, as in the Protestant Reformation type, on seeking the inward conversion of individual people to an affective faith. Rather, it is expressed through Christian people offering themselves to the local indigenous community, whatever that happens to be, so that they may give and receive hospitality and care and so that genuine dialogue and witness may take place. In this way they believe and hope that the healing, forgiving and transforming love of Christ, a sign of the kingdom which unites the sacred and the secular, will be known in that place. Mission, then, is all about finding this kind of hope in local communities (see Figure 8). (See Morisy 2004 for exploration of this kind of mission through church community projects.)

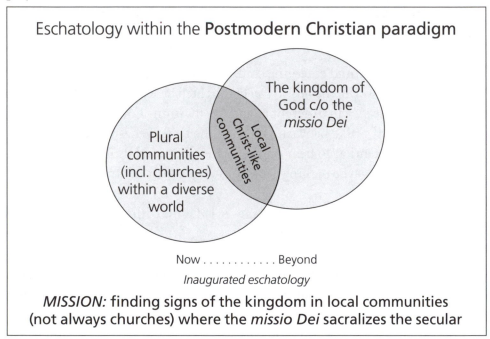

Eschatology within the **Postmodern Christian paradigm**

The kingdom of God c/o the *missio Dei*

Plural communities (incl. churches) within a diverse world

Local Christ-like communities

Now . . . . Beyond

Inaugurated eschatology

MISSION: finding signs of the kingdom in local communities (not always churches) where the *missio Dei* sacralizes the secular

Figure 8

(Note: Robert Schreiter has recently argued that the Christian work of seeking reconciliation and healing in the trouble-spots of the world provides a contemporary postmodern paradigm of mission. This is because of the way many churches and agencies have sponsored this work in many parts of the world in the last fifty years (see Schreiter 2005; see also Mellor and Yates 2004). This is an important argument and reflects widespread ecumenical thinking. However, it does not necessarily reflect church life at local level, which is only occasionally involved in social and political peacemaking. Local mission today in many places seems much less focused and more open to a range of issues and concerns, which is why this *Studyguide* uses a more generalized typological description for postmodern mission.)

Summary of the postmodern Christian paradigm

Context
The Holocaust, atomic bomb, poverty, oppression, pluralism, postmodernism, ecological crisis (i.e. the failure of the Enlightenment project).

Authority
Contextual 'particular' experience
and tradition/scripture.

Methodology
Action-reflection: the pastoral cycle of experience, exploration, reflection, and action.

Eschatology
God is bringing liberation for all the world at the end (the missio Dei) – first fruits of this kingdom can be experienced here and now by those who seek it.

Christology
Christ's mission is found through Scripture and identification with the culture of the place, whether traditional or postmodern: incarnational.

Discipleship

Reflection – listening to God through particular experience, Scripture and tradition.

Action – conforming daily living to the kingdom of God here and now.

Mission of the Church

To be a locally rooted community of hospitality and care, prophetically pointing to the coming of the kingdom.

Ministry

To nurture this community in theological, personal and practical ways, i.e. to be a practical community theologian.

Some examples

Barth, Bonhoeffer, Vincent Donovan, emerging churches.

Debate

Galilean principles of the *missio Christi* (from p. 33)

1. Contemplative listening, which frames all ministry: listening to God, to other people, to oneself, especially in times of prayer and retreat.

2. Addressing society as a whole, at points where people live and work, including and especially the marginalized. This results in being received and accepted by some but rejected and opposed by others.

3. Pointing to the inaugurated yet still awaited kingdom, in word and in surprising saving deed (symbolic actions) which address the actual needs of people (both individual and structural); but without publicizing the wonders.

4. Calling for a personal response by all to the coming of this kingdom.

5. Doing all this through a collaborative team, who themselves are powerless and vulnerable and must suffer the consequences.

One response

1. It has been clear throughout this chapter that *listening* has been central to the development of this type of mission. It was present at the beginning when Barth listened to the fact that the theology he inherited had nothing to say to the workers in Safenwil and that, at the same time, the Bible was speaking to him out of a strange and different world. It was present in Bonhoeffer when, in his prison cell, he faced up to the way the modern world no longer had need of traditional religion ('man's coming of age') and that Christian mission and ministry should now be all about the vulnerability of service rather than the strength of domination. It was clearly apparent in Donovan's method of evangelism, which involved asking questions and listening to the Masai before beginning to speak of the gospel. And in the emerging church movement, as we have just seen, a deep openness to postmodern culture is a foundation of all that happens.

2. This type of mission is clearly located within contemporary urban culture. It seeks to make contact with anyone and everyone who lives within it. It therefore fulfils the second Galilean principle: it is fundamentally an attempt to serve God's mission at the point where people live and work. However, there is a limitation, in that the plural nature of contemporary society, with its 'incommensurability' and 'difference', means that identification with one group prevents identification with another. Older generations who live in the suburbs or country areas, for example, do not seem to figure very prominently in the life of emerging churches.

There are attempts to overcome this. The Fresh Expressions initiative within the UK, an officially sponsored attempt to gather information and promote new forms of the Church, uses a much wider definition of a church: it is seeking to promote forms of church 'established primarily for the benefit of people who are not yet members of any church' (*Fresh Expressions* 2006, p. 2). These include new types of services within existing churches, church community projects, forms of chaplaincy within educational institutions, and worship activities for children. But by the same token, the wider definition loses the distinctiveness of the postmodern mission type, which as we have just seen emphasizes vulnerability, dialogue with witness, and uniting the sacred and secular. In its understandable desire to be inclusive the Fresh Expressions initiative loses its focus on what is new and distinctive about emerging churches.

It remains an open question, then, as to whether this type of mission can address society as a whole. Its concern for the marginalized, however, is clear: they are central to its being: 'On one occasion our community was getting kicked out of a park because of our interaction with the homeless. "You can't feed the homeless here; you need a permit," the policeman said. I replied, "We are not feeding the homeless. We are having a picnic. We're eating with them"' (Spencer Burke in Gibbs and Bolger 2006, p. 135).

3. Does this mission type point to the kingdom of God? There was no doubt in the mind of the Masai Christian who described what God had done through Donovan as being like a lion embracing its prey. The proleptic relationship of church life to the kingdom of God is also a strong theme within the emerging church movement. Gibbs and Bolger report that in emerging churches the 'direction' of church life changed from being a centripetal dynamic (flowing in) to a centrifugal dynamic. 'This in turn led to a shift in emphasis from attracting crowds to equipping, dispersing, and multiplying Christ followers as a central function of the church.' They then quote Andrew Jones, who provides a theological explanation of what they mean:

> Emerging churches should be missional. And by missional, I understand that the emerging church will take shape inside the new culture as a redeeming prophetic influence. The church follows the kingdom, the church happens in *their* house rather than *our* house, just as it did in Matthew's house, and in Lydia's house, or the home of Priscilla and Aquila. The motion is always centrifugal, flowing outward to bring reconciliation and blessing to where it is needed. (Gibbs and Bolger 2006, p. 51)

Furthermore, emerging churches do not just use words to bear witness to what they believe. Another feature of their life is eating together, an action which demonstrates the hospitality and care that is so important to them. This can be seen in Spencer Burke's quotation above. For some of the churches this dimension has led to a restoration of the centrality of the Eucharist to their life (ibid., pp. 228–9).

4. Do emerging churches call for a personal response by all to the coming of the kingdom? Karen Ward's rejection of overt evangelism, quoted on p. 179 above,

would suggest that they do not. There is no direct challenge to people to make a decision for or against what is presented. However, her words also make clear that an evangelistic call does takes place implicitly, through the quality of the life of the Christian community: 'We are to love one another, and that creates its own attraction. Taking care of the sick and the needy creates all the evangelism we need.' For some this will be enough. But will it be enough for everyone? The suspicion here is that postmodern mission might be too reticent about engaging in the kind of evangelism which impels people to make a definite choice and commit themselves one way or the other. On occasion the fourth Galilean principle will struggle to find expression in this mission type.

5. A collaborative approach to leadership is a key part of the emerging church culture, as the eighth common practice shows. Of all the types of mission this is one that embodies this most clearly and impressively. It is always possible that at a future point certain key leaders or gurus will come to the fore and direct the future course of the movement. At the moment, thankfully, none seem to have done so and Gibbs and Bolger's book shows there are many different people involved in 'the conversation' which is taking this movement forward in innovative and exciting ways (see especially chapter 10).

Discussion questions

Are there local contexts where this type of mission may *not* be what is needed?
Why do you think this?
What might the strengths and weaknesses of this type of mission be within your own local context?

Further reading

Barth, Karl (1933), *The Epistle to the Romans*, Oxford University Press
Barth, Karl (1956), *Church Dogmatics, vol. I: The Doctrine of the Word of God*, T & T Clark
Bauman, Zygmunt (2005) *Liquid Life*, Polity Press

Bevans, Stephen B., and Roger P. Schroeder (2004), *Constants in Context: A Theology of Mission for Today*, Orbis

Bonhoeffer, Dietrich (1959), *Letters and Papers from Prison*, Fontana

Bosch, David J. (1992), *Transforming Mission: Paradigm Shifts in Theology of Mission*, Orbis

Bradstock, Andrew, and Christopher Rowland, eds (2002), *Radical Christian Writings: A Reader*, Blackwell

Donovan, Vincent (1982), *Christianity Rediscovered: An Epistle from the Masai*, SCM Press

Dulles, Avery, SJ (1988), *Models of the Church*, 2nd edn, Gill & Macmillan

Fresh Expressions: Prospectus Phase 2 (2006), Fresh Expressions Ltd

Gallagher, Michael (2003), *Clashing Symbols: An Introduction to Faith and Culture*, rev. edn, DLT

Gibbs, Eddie, and Ryan K. Bolger (2006), *Emerging Churches: Creating Christian Community in Postmodern Culture*, SPCK

Harvey, David (1991), *The Condition of Postmodernity: An Enquiry into the Origins of Cultural Change*, Blackwell

Healey, Joseph G., and Jeanne Hinton, eds (2005), *Small Christian Communities Today: Capturing the New Moment*, Orbis

Iggers, George G. (1968), *The German Conception of History*, Wesleyan University Press

Jenkins, Philip (2002), *The Next Christendom: The Coming of Global Christianity*, Oxford University Press

Jenson, Robert W. (1997), in David Ford, ed., *The Modern Theologians*, 2nd edn, Blackwell

Küng, Hans (1995), *Christianity: Its Essence and History*, SCM Press

Mellor, Howard, and Timothy Yates, eds (2004), *Mission, Violence and Reconciliation*, Cliff College Publishing

Middleton, J. Richard, and Brian J. Walsh (1995), *Truth is Stranger than it Used to Be: Biblical Faith in a Postmodern Age*, Part One, 'The Postmodern Condition', SPCK

Morisy, Ann (2004), *Journeying Out: A New Approach to Christian Mission*, Continuum

Sanneh, Lamin (1989), *Translating the Message: The Missionary Impact on Culture*, Orbis

Schreiter, Robert J. (2005), 'Reconciliation and Healing as a Paradigm for Mission', *International Review of Mission* vol. 94 (January)

Smith, David (2003), *Mission after Christendom*, DLT

Stuart Hughes, H. (1979), *Consciousness and Society: The Reorientation of European Social Thought 1890–1930*, Harvester Press

Vanier, Jean (1988), 'The Basis of Dialogue', from *The Broken Body: Journey to Wholeness*, DLT

Walls, Andrew F. (1996), *The Missionary Movement in Christian History: Studies in the Transmission of Faith*, Orbis

Ward, Pete (2002) *Liquid Church*, Paternoster Press

Wingate, Andrew (2005), *Celebrating Difference, Staying Faithful: How to Live in a Multi-faith World*, DLT

World Council of Churches (1979), *Guidelines on Dialogue with People of Living Faiths and Ideologies*, WCC

Conclusion

Which Type of Mission?

All this he showed me with great joy, saying,
'See, I am God. See I am in all things.
See, I do all things.
See, I never take my hands off my work,
nor ever shall, through all eternity.
See, I lead all things to the end I have prepared for them.
I do this by the same wisdom and love and power
through which I made them.
How can anything be done that is not well done?'

Mother Julian of Norwich

This *Studyguide* began its explorations with the recent rediscovery of the concept of *missio Dei* in Western theology, the insight that authentic mission is not owned or manufactured by the churches but flows from the heart of God himself, beginning with his creation of the world, reaching its definitive expression in the incarnation, death and resurrection of Christ, and continuing since Pentecost through the agency of the Holy Spirit in the Church and in the world. But the *missio Dei* will only be complete at the end of all things (as Mother Julian says), at the eschaton, when his kingdom will unite all things in heaven and earth. The Church does not own or control this mission but is privileged to participate in it as a sign and agent of transformation.

We then explored the way in which mission is grounded in the life of God and were led into discussions of the doctrine of the Trinity. Following recent scholarly debate of this doctrine we saw that the Trinity is a participative relationship in which Father, Son and Holy Spirit give and receive their identities from each other: they are not three independently existing individuals who enter into a relationship with each other, but three interdependent beings who form a unity through their giving and receiving. This 'coinherence' provides a point of connection with mission, for mission is the outpouring of this dance-like life into the world, inviting and drawing others to share in its life-giving exchange.

Christian mission, then, cannot be a one-way relationship in which one person simply gives something to someone else. Nor can it be a two-way relationship in which two parties enter into an exchange of gifts just between themselves. It must involve a three-way relationship, where what is exchanged between two parties is also exchanged with a third and in which this giving and receiving is mutually upholding and overflowing.

To see what this means in human terms we turned to the Galilean ministry of Jesus and with the aid of contemporary scholarship attempted to identify its key features. We saw how three key players could be identified in the unfolding drama: first, the society in which and to which Jesus addressed his mission; second, the incoming and transforming reality of the kingdom of God, whose arrival had been inaugurated but not yet completed; and third, Jesus and his followers, whose prophetic ministry was all about announcing the second of these players to the first.

We can now see that the interaction of these three players shows a correspondence with the interaction of the three persons of the Trinity: Jesus' identity was constituted by his interaction with both Jewish society and the incoming kingdom; the kingdom gained its identity from the ministry of Jesus as well as from its object, which was Jewish society as large; and that society, in so far as it paid attention to Jesus and opened itself to the coming of the kingdom, had its identity transformed by them.

We were also able to identify some of the practical principles underlying Jesus' mission. Through exegesis of Mark 1 we were able to name five *Galilean principles* that guided the mission of Jesus and his followers. These principles then guided the subsequent assessment of different historic approaches to mission.

The main chapters of this *Studyguide* then presented six ways in which the Christian community has continued to express the mission of Christ through different periods of history and in different cultural contexts. This presentation was based on the historical overview of Christian history in the work of

David Tracey and Hans Küng, and of mission history in the work of David J. Bosch. This presentation identified six distinct 'types' of mission that have guided Christian missionary practice over the centuries: filling the Ark, radiating eternal truth, establishing Christendom, the conversion of souls, building the kingdom on earth, and finding hope in local communities. Certain theologians, church leaders and movements were used to unpack and illustrate the key features of each. Then, using the five Galilean principles drawn from the biblical exegesis, each type was assessed to see how far it expressed contemporary understanding of the mission of Christ. Some of the types fared better than others in this assessment. The point, though, was not to dismiss some or all of them, but to come to an understanding of the strengths and weaknesses of each for a comprehensive understanding of Christian mission.

As mentioned in the Preface, local churches have only limited resources and cannot expect to inhabit and express all types of mission. A Christian community, listening to God and listening to its neighbours, needs to discover which is the mission type that it can inhabit in this place at this time. This will be influenced by the character of the local context and the needs and opportunities it presents. The gathering of this information can take as much or as little time as is available. Surveys, questionnaires, searches of parish records and government statistical data, interviews and analysis of social and economic trends can all play a part. Initial impressions of an area are also valuable. Analysis of how the churches of the area relate to their surroundings is also important. A good place to begin is through conducting an audit of the area and of the place of the church within it (see Ballard and Pritchard 2006 for an easy-to-use example; see Cameron *et al.* 2005 for further guidance and bibliographies). Out of this study will come an awareness of which mission types are practical options for this church and its people at this time.

But then, returning to our starting point, decisions about Christian outreach need to be based on what God is already doing in that place, on how the *missio Dei* is at work in that context. Christian participation in mission needs to have as its foundation a profound openness to this wider and deeper dimension: it needs to be open to what the Spirit is doing in the world, so that it may enter into that divine movement of exchange. As H. Richard Niebuhr wrote with reference to Christian ethics, the first question is not 'What should I do?' but 'What is going on here?'

Rosa Parks, with whom we began, was someone rooted in Scripture and in the Baptist tradition and who had a strong sense that God's mission was concerned with racial justice and human rights for blacks as well as whites. She knew she had a small but important role in that movement. Martin Luther King Junior also understood the prophetic nature of what she and the whole civil rights movement were doing. She provided the prophetic sign of what was coming and he provided the prophetic words that explained and guided it all. Out of their listening came their participation in a powerful missionary movement.

Every Christian is called to listen to God in Scripture and tradition but not every Christian or local church is called to such dramatic forms of participation. For many to be faithful to the *missio Dei* means something much more ordinary, a simple listening to the other on a one-to-one basis. What does this involve?

Jean Vanier is someone who provides real help, writing out of his experience in the L'Arche communities. These are small residential communities which enable people with learning disabilities to live with others who help them and learn from them (see Spink 2006). Vanier has written that 'if you wish to enter the world of those who are broken or closed in upon themselves, it is important to learn their language'. He then draws out what this actually means:

> Learning a language is not just learning French or Spanish or German. It is learning to understand what people are really saying, the non-verbal as well as the verbal language. The verbal, exterior language is the beginning and is absolutely necessary, but you must go deeper and discover what it means to listen: to listen deeply to another, to the cry flowing from the heart, in order to understand people, both in their pain and in their gift; to understand what they are truly asking so that you can hold their wound, their pain and all that flows from it: violence, anger or depression, self-centredness and limitless demands; the suffocating urge to possess, the refusal to let go; to accept these with compassion, without judging, without condemning. (Vanier 1988, pp. 80–1)

Vanier also describes how this communication takes place not only through words but through the language of the body:

> To do this means you must listen and understand the non-verbal language of the body as well as the language of words. The first language of the child is so deep, this language of the body. We can perhaps recognize the pain and

anguish conveyed in the taut face, all screwed up, of a tiny baby, just as we can recognize the peaceful surrender in its radiance of trust and light. Some people can only talk with their bodies; only from there do true words flow . . . (ibid., p. 81)

Vanier then, significantly, recalls that on the Day of Pentecost the disciples were given the ability to communicate in different languages. This was 'so that they might understand, right from the beginning, the ways of God'. These ways, which are the ways of mission, are then spelled out by Vanier in a clear, concise and definitive way:

He wants us to respect difference and to learn the language of the other so that there may be true communication and communion . . . Learn and respect others in their own culture; their ways of eating, their ways of inter- acting, their ways of doing things, their forms of relationships. Come, listen and learn. Do not judge others and their ways; instead respect them and love them. (ibid., p. 82)

Finally, significantly, Vanier describes how this way of approaching the other begins to open up the heart of mission, for 'if you come in this way, open, lis- tening humbly, without judging, then gradually you will discover that you are trusted. Your heart will be touched.'

This mission, though, is more than our own attempts to reach out to others: it is a greater and inclusive mission: 'You will begin to discover the secret of communion' (ibid., pp. 82–3).

Behind such communication lies something else, a deeper unity which allows the one to commune with the other. This is the unity that comes from God and which the quotation from Mother Julian at the start of this chapter described. It is a unity present in the way God leads all things to 'the end I have prepared for them'. The Christian community, as it commits itself to serving the *missio Dei*, can open itself to this leadership and allow his 'wisdom and love and power' to infuse and transform its own life.

Thomas Merton (1915–68), the Trappist monk, mystic and writer, provides a vivid picture of how this can happen. It comes from one of his journals from the early 1960s and, in its inviting simplicity, provides a fitting conclusion to this book:

In Louisville, at the corner of Fourth and Walnut, in the centre of the shopping district, I was suddenly overwhelmed with the realization that I loved all those people, that they were mine and I theirs, that we could not be alien to one another even though we were total strangers. It was like waking from a dream of separateness, of spurious self-isolation in a special world, the world of renunciation and supposed holiness . . . This sense of liberation from an illusory difference was such a relief and such a joy to me that I almost laughed out loud. And I suppose my happiness could have taken form in the words 'Thank God, thank God that I *am* like other men, that I am only a man among others' . . . Then it was as if I suddenly saw the secret beauty of their hearts, the depths of their hearts where neither sin nor desire nor self-knowledge can reach, the core of their reality, the person that each one is in God's eyes . . . It is like pure diamond, blazing with the invisible light of heaven. It is in everybody, and if we could see it we would see these billions of points of light coming together in the face and blaze of a sun that would make all the darkness and cruelty of life vanish completely . . . I have no program for this seeing. It is only given. But the gate of heaven is everywhere. (Merton 1995, pp. 156–8)

Discussion questions

What would encourage your church community to open itself to the leadership of the *missio Dei*?
How could your church community respond in practical ways?

Further reading

Ballard, Paul, and John Pritchard (2006), *Practical Theology in Action*, 2nd edn, SPCK

Cameron, Helen, *et al.*, eds (2005), *Studying Local Churches: A Handbook*, SCM Press

Merton, Thomas (1995), *Conjectures of a Guilty Bystander*, Burns & Oates

Spink, Kathryn (2006), *The Miracle, the Message, the Story: Jean Vanier and L'Arche*, DLT

Vanier, Jean (1988), *The Broken Body: Journey to Wholeness*, DLT

Epilogue

The Coming of the Rains

How can the *missio Dei* be visualized? In one sense this is an easy question to answer because Jesus Christ is 'the image of the invisible God' and therefore the *missio Christi* represents the *missio Dei*. But in another sense, if we want an image of God's mission at work through the ebb and flow of history, it is very difficult to provide an answer. The previous chapters have described a rich variety of ways in which the Christian churches have participated in that mission, indicating that God's missionary activity itself has been richly diverse and complex.

A metaphor will have to do, because this does not attempt to represent every aspect of its object but just to convey some key features through an image that is otherwise unrelated to it. In the following pages one extended metaphor is presented with some reflections on how it represents the *missio Dei*. It is a metaphor that is able to represent both God's initiative and sovereignty in mission, which is the outpouring of his Trinitarian life bringing the salvation of his kingdom to the world, *and* the important and creative role of human response to that, which we have seen especially in the different paradigms of Christian life through the centuries.

The metaphor comes from Southern Africa and is centred on the coming of the rains after a long dry season. Anyone who has lived in that part of the world will know that this is an awesome experience.

Gift

Before the rains come there is a steady and relentless build up of heat. The vegetation becomes dry and brittle. The earth becomes powdery sand and a fine dust settles over everything. One can sense how every living thing from the smallest shrub to the largest mammal longs for the moist relief the rain will bring. Then, after several months without proper rain, something in the atmosphere changes and the sky becomes hazy and the air humid. The first clear signs of change are often the thorn trees in the bush which can suddenly and magically burst into a bright golden blossom, this taking place long before any drops of rain have actually fallen. The tree wisterias and, in the towns, the jacarandas soon follow, clothing themselves with an advent purple blossom. Yet the build-up of heat continues and with it increasing discomfort and yearning for relief. One begins to examine the shape and density of the clouds, looking, often vainly, for tell-tale signs of rain. In some years there can be a prolonged pre-rainy season, when the clouds tower up impressively overhead but release nothing onto the earth.

Finally, however, something happens in the air currents and the clouds begin to reach across and dominate the whole sky, blotting out the sun. Gusts of wind suddenly whip up the trees, the cloud cover becomes dark and heavy and, her-alded by a jubilant crack of thunder, the heavens at last open and the rain begins to fall. In a good year the rain will start gradually and continue for a whole day or night, soothing and soaking the earth, turning dusty sand into damp soil and releasing an expectant moist aroma. At that moment a surge of excitement ripples through everyone and children will rush out into the first rains and leap and jump around in them. There is a strong sense of new life returning to the earth and of the miracle of growth beginning once more.

Then the growth begins. First tiny new shoots of grass appear in the soil and quickly begin to push upwards. They soon create what seems like a bright green carpet that spreads over the whole land. The bushes and trees unfurl their tender new leaves in a bright array of yellows, bronzes and gold. In the fields the brown earth is transformed into a riot of competing weeds and grasses.

The rains, then, come of their own accord and in their own time, majestically inaugurating the season of growth. They cannot be controlled by the people who live on and *off* the land. In this way they are like the coming of the king-dom which is primarily God's work and not human work. The kingdom comes about as a result of his majestic initiative and in his own time: this is what Jesus showed when he came into Galilee proclaiming that the kingdom of God was at hand. He did this after the long period in which the people of Israel were told of the coming of the messiah by the prophets and looked forward to that event but did not know when and how it would take place.

And then the rains, when they fall, fall on everyone, good and bad alike, committed farmer and lazy farmer alike. All receive the free gift they bring, the gift of life and the promise of plenty to come. In the same way, what Christ brings is for the whole world and, indeed, for the whole of creation: it is 'a plan for the fullness of time, to unite all things in him, things in heaven and things on earth' (Ephesians 1.9–10). In response to this the kingdom is offered to everyone: 'Go . . . and invite . . . as many as you find.'

Response

The subsistence farmer knows that what she needs more than anything else has now arrived. But she does not rest. The coming of the rains does not on its own produce the much-needed crops but, rather, promises such crops to the farmer prepared to commit herself to cultivation. She must harness her plough to her oxen or donkeys and begin the work of preparing her fields for seed. She must carefully plant, making sure there is enough space between each individual seed. Slowly but persistently the weeds must be removed and the pests resisted. The coming of the rains means the coming of the hard work of cultivation if those rains are to be turned into food for the table.

Furthermore, during the rainy season no one can be sure when the rains will continue to fall, when the sun will shine and when growth and finally the harvest will be ready. Sensitivity and patience are needed by the farmer to allow her crops to mature in their own time. She should not reap them too early. In the same way the timing of the growth of the fruits of salvation within the believer and within the community of faith cannot be known in advance, nor the ways that they will actually come about. The *promise* of salvation is known from the beginning: all who respond to God should know that they will receive the fullness of salvation, and so in this sense they are already saved (or, put in different terms, they are already justified). But the actual growth of that salvation in their lives, through the growth of the fruits of health in mind, body and spirit, takes place in its own time and own way: 'Be patient, therefore, brethren, until the coming of the Lord. Behold, the farmer waits for the precious fruit of the earth, being patient over it until it receives the early and the late rain. You also be patient' (James 5.7). Furthermore, the timing of the completion of the whole is not yet known: 'But of that day or that hour no one knows . . . Take heed, watch, for you do not know when the time will come' (Mark 13.32–3). And so the metaphor shows how the full reality of salvation is yet to come.

Different farmers respond to the rains in different ways. Some, indeed most, plant maize and then cultivate and harvest that crop. Others, especially in the drier areas of Southern Africa, plant sorghum and millet, which are more drought-resistant. They then cultivate and reap those crops. Others with access to irrigation concentrate on vegetables. So all the farmers respond to the promise of the rains, and eventually are given life and health by those rains, but respond in a variety of ways. In the same way we have seen through the historic paradigms how Christians have responded to the *missio Dei* in a rich variety of ways and with a rich variety of outcomes.

Again, cultivation is not a quick process. It takes several months of work for the fields to produce their crops. Some crops are quicker than others but all need a persistent attention over time if they are to produce good yields. In the same way, the cultivation of new ways of living, of prayer, Bible study, worship, giving, service of the community, and so on, have all taken time to become part of the life of the Church: the paradigms have taken time to establish themselves. The longer-term view must be taken.

Some subsistence farmers do not respond at all to the coming of the rains. For a variety of reasons, sometimes including the vain hope that they will simply be given the food they need by relatives or by some donor agency, they do nothing. Sometimes they are too busy with other things, whether looking for work or working elsewhere. A journey around the communal areas in mid-season will always reveal a number of fields where the ground has not been ploughed and no crops are growing. In the same way, of course, many did not respond to Christ and do not respond to the coming of God's reign: 'And they rose up and put him out of the city . . .' (Luke 4.29). The free gift Christ offers often falls to the ground because many have not opened their hands to receive it. For whatever reason the grace of salvation is ignored: 'He came to his own home, and his own people received him not' (John 1.11).

Finally, in their own time, when they are ready, the crops can be gathered in, the maize cobs stripped of their soft green coverings and placed in the pot. The promise seen in the coming of the advent blossom and the first rains is at last fulfilled in the serving of a nutritious meal to a hungry family. With the farmer's commitment, wisdom and hard work the rains have borne their plentiful fruits. Similarly, the believer and the community of faith will come to experience a new life, the life of salvation, in liberation, in healing, in forgiveness and reconciliation, and in peace. These things come in God's time and are not made or constructed by human hands. They are the fulfilment and culmination of the *missio Dei*.

Index